Lebanon

The Politics of Revolving Doors

THE WASHINGTON PAPERS

. . . intended to meet the need for an authoritative, yet prompt, public appraisal of the major developments in world affairs.

Series Editors: Walter Laqueur; Amos A. Jordan

Associate Editors: William J. Taylor, Jr.; M. Jon Vondracek

Executive Editor: Jean C. Newsom

Managing Editor: Nancy B. Eddy

MANUSCRIPT SUBMISSION

The Washington Papers and Praeger Publishers welcome inquiries concerning manuscript submissions. Please include with your inquiry a curriculum vita, synopsis, table of contents, and estimated manuscript length. Submissions to *The Washington Papers* should be sent to *The Washington Papers*; The Center for Strategic and International Studies; Georgetown University; 1800 K Street NW; Suite 400; Washington, DC 20006. Book proposals should be sent to Praeger Publishers; 521 Fifth Avenue; New York NY 10175.

The Washington Papers/114

Lebanon

The Politics of Revolving Doors

Wadi D. Haddad

Foreword by Donald Rumsfeld

Published with The Center for
Strategic and International Studies,
Georgetown University, Washington, D.C.

PRAEGER SPECIAL STUDIES • PRAEGER SCIENTIFIC

Library of Congress Cataloging in Publication Data

Haddad, Wadi.
  Lebanon, the politics of revolving doors.

  (The Washington papers, ISSN 0278-937X ;
v. XIII, 114)
  "Published with the Center for Strategic and
International Studies, Georgetown University,
Washington, D.C."
  Bibliography: p.
  1. Lebanon – Politics and government – 1975–
I. Georgetown University. Center for Strategic and
International Studies. II. Series: Washington
papers ; vol. XIII, 114.

DS87.H29 1985   320.95692   85-6511
ISBN 0-03-005539-3
ISBN 0-03-005542-3 (pbk.)

The *Washington Papers* are written under the auspices of The Center
for Strategic and International Studies (CSIS), Georgetown University
and published with CSIS by Praeger Publishers. The views expressed in these
papers are those of the authors and not necessarily those of The Center.

Published in 1985 by Praeger Publishers
CBS Educational and Professional Publishing, a Division of CBS Inc.
521 Fifth Avenue, New York, NY 10175 USA

Printed in the United States of America on acid-free paper

INTERNATIONAL OFFICES

Orders from outside the United States should be sent to the appropriate address listed below. Orders
from areas not listed below should be placed through CBS International Publishing, 383 Madison Ave.,
New York, NY 10175 USA

Australia, New Zealand
Holt Saunders, Pty, Ltd., 9 Waltham St., Artarmon, N.S.W. 2064, Sydney, Australia
Canada
Holt, Rinehart & Winston of Canada, 55 Horner Ave., Toronto, Ontario, Canada M8Z 4X6
Europe, the Middle East, & Africa
Holt Saunders, Ltd., 1 St. Anne's Road, Eastbourne, East Sussex, England BN21 3UN
Japan
Holt Saunders, Ltd., Ichibancho Central Building, 22-1 Ichibancho, 3rd Floor, Chiyodaku, Tokyo, Japan
Hong Kong, Southeast Asia
Holt Saunders Asia, Ltd., 10 Fl, Intercontinental Plaza, 94 Granville Road, Tsim Sha Tsui East,
Kowloon, Hong Kong

**Manuscript submissions should be sent to the Editorial Director, Praeger Publishers, 521 Fifth Avenue,
New York, NY 10175 USA**

Contents

Foreword

Dr. Wadi Haddad brings a special perspective to this useful analysis of the tragedy that has engulfed Lebanon, combining his analytical tools as a scholar with his unique vantage point as President Gemayel's national security adviser during the 18 critical months ending in May, 1984.

As the U.S. special representative for the Middle East during the latter portion of that period, I came to know Dr. Haddad and to appreciate his deep commitment to his country and its people, his determination to find workable answers to exceedingly complex problems, his courage in forcefully setting forth his views even when not in conformance with current thinking, and his willingness to face personal risks of every kind. His paper reflects many of these admirable qualities.

Dr. Haddad objectively, and often starkly, describes the storms that have buffeted the fragile Lebanese state. One need only reflect on events of recent years to sense the magnitude of the problem:

- the influx of Palestinians in the early 1970s,
- the entry of the Arab Deterrent Force in the mid-1970s,
- the disequilibrium in the Arab world,

- the invasion of Lebanon by Israeli forces and their subsequent withdrawal from the Shouf,
- the assassination of key Lebanese leaders,
- the presence and then withdrawal of the Multinational Force,
- the growing influence of radical Khomeini supporters,
- the inability to provide minimal security even in the capital city,
- the success of the use of disruptive surrogates, armed and funded from the outside, and
- the "terror" resulting from the successful use of externally sponsored terrorist acts.

He sensitively traces the roots of Lebanon's confessional problems and the repeated efforts to strike a balance, the formula for which has confounded so many for so long. Anyone dealing with the Lebanese factions cannot help but be struck by the degree to which confessionalism affects all aspects of Lebanese politics.

The tragedy is that deep seated mistrust, some of it admittedly well placed, leads inexorably to a posturing, delaying game by the parties in the hope of an improved position, while ignoring the reality that time and continued conflict damage the positions of all, particularly the Lebanese people.

Dr. Haddad understandably offers no panacea for Lebanon's problems. He notes that any attempt to deal with his country's ills will necessitate a painful surgical procedure, cutting through layers of Lebanon's scars.

He argues that Lebanon, perhaps because it is weaker than its neighbors, has often been a victim of the hostility among its neighbors. It has become a participant in the regional conflict, not as a player, but rather the terrain over which a portion of that struggle has and is being contested. Unlike many, however, he correctly refuses to ascribe Lebanon's continuing predicament solely to the machinations of outside forces.

He properly points out that weakness is provocative, that the absence of strength and the inability to assure order invited disorder. The inability to provide security, even for the capital, points up the truth that sovereignty, without the ability to defend it, is at the sufferance of others.

Dr. Haddad's view from the perspective of his past work on Lebanese public policy is particularly useful. Surely the insights of any participant are more complete where they discuss events from their particular vantage point. Surely other participants – the various Lebanese factions, other Arab States, Israel, the members of the Multinational Force – saw some of the events described through somewhat different lenses, as did I. So although his represents an important perspective, it probably will be enriched by other perspectives as history unfolds.

Dr. Haddad refuses to accept the demise of Lebanon. Rather, he argues that Lebanon has been going through a traumatic maturation process as it struggles to establish the optimal formula that will reflect its diversity and still provide stability. It has been said that the rise and fall of nations depends in major part on a capacity for collective action. If that is true, as I believe it to be, it may yet take a catalytic event or a new generation of leaders to provide that vital dynamic.

In the last analysis the future of Lebanon and the prospects for an end to this protracted conflict will depend on the interaction of powerful competing ideas, the facts on the ground, and the contributions of dedicated individuals of all persuasions. All who have seen the brutalization of the people of Lebanon pray for the success of those working to restore peace and freedom to this troubled, exhausted, but still amazingly vital people.

It is a tribute to Dr. Haddad and others in Lebanon who have worked under constant pressure and life-threatening conditions that they persist in their dedication and efforts toward their vision.

Donald Rumsfeld
the President's Personal Representative
to the Middle East (1983-1984)

Preface

This is neither a book of memoirs nor a history; it is an attempt to provide a brief but comprehensive analysis of the nature and evolution of the Lebanese conflict, the dynamics of the forces that have interacted in the process of resolving it, and the prospects for the future. The issues and developments are those I have wrestled with in the course of two experiences in Lebanese public life. Because the identity and conceptualization of issues and events are themselves subject to dispute, I have sought to approach them by comparing and examining the respective policies and roles of all major actors in the Lebanese tragedy in the context of initiatives, negotiations, and discussions – some in the glare of the public spotlight, others in the shadow of secrecy. Implicit in this approach is the importance of interpretation in selecting and conceptualizing the issues, which were often buried in rhetoric, in establishing the interaction between events, in ordering the discussions to highlight the issues, and in explicating the positions to make them comprehensible to the reader.

I have benefited from the advice and assistance of many friends and colleagues in the preparation of this text. I am particularly indebted to Edward E. Azar, director of the Center for International Development at the University of Maryland, for his contribution to the conceptual structuring of my thoughts and his intellectual and political critique of my ideas and interpretations. His friendship and good judgement have been invaluable. I am also grateful to Ron McLaurin for his specific editorial assistance and suggestions and to the staff at the Georgetown University Center for Strategic and International Studies for their courtesy and assistance in the processing of the manuscript. Several other people have read the manuscript and given me insightful comments, many of which I have used with appreciation. Any shortcomings that remain in a necessarily interpretive work are my own.

Washington, D.C.
January 1985

About the Author

Wadi D. Haddad is a private consultant and an adjunct fellow at Georgetown University's Center for Strategic and International Studies. Between December 1982 and May 1984 he was heavily involved in Lebanese politics as adviser to the president of Lebanon for national security and policy affairs. Prior to that he was education adviser and chief of the Western Africa Education Projects Division at the World Bank (1976–1982); president-director general of the National Center for Educational Research and Development in Lebanon (1972–1976); and professor and director of the Science and Mathematics Education Center at the American University of Beirut (1967–1972). Dr. Haddad was educated at the American University of Beirut and received his Ph.D. from the University of Wisconsin. He is the author of many books and articles in the various areas of science and education.

Lebanon

The Politics of Revolving Doors

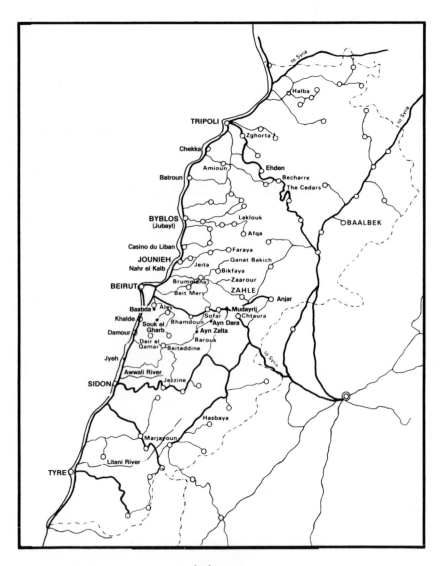

Lebanon

I

The Nature of the Lebanese Conflict

1

Introduction

When violence erupted in Lebanon in April 1975 and the first phase of the conflict spread in Beirut, a host of explanations was offered. From that time to the present a wide variety of theories has been advanced as appropriate to understanding the violence or as necessary to reducing it. The passage of time and the kaleidoscopic portrait that has emerged from this period suggest that the "conflict" in Lebanon has been in fact a complex of several conflicts and that time has heightened the interaction and interdependence of the several components. Nor do the several conflicts lie on a single plane; they are of quite different types, producing a conflict vortex the elements of which are multidimensional as well as interactive.

A remarkable aspect of the problems in Lebanon is the difficulty in delimiting them. If the conflict is internal, as some aver, how do we explain the role of Israel, Syria, the Arab world, the United States, and the Arab-Israeli issue – all of which have had a far-reaching impact in Lebanon? Yet to define the conflict as regional or international submerges the real and great differences within Lebanon that have quite on their own generated a substantial volume of violence, death, and destruction.

Protracted conflicts such as the Lebanese tragedy that

involve whole societies are not easy to disentangle. They seem to grow in complexity and cost as time and events go by. Protraction acts like a magnet for problems, and the difficulties tend to acquire new causes and new participants that only further impede conflict reduction, resolution, and termination. Conflicts of this type therefore tend to acquire a momentum of their own and generate more rigid images of the process and structure of the conflict.

Societally based protracted conflicts victimize every party — the elites, the masses, and both external and internal forces. They assume and consume. They encourage stereotyping and rigidity; they discourage careful analysis, defy clear communication, and defeat credible solutions. Their multidimensionality impedes the search for acceptable confidence-building measures. That is why the art and science of conflict resolution must deal with the constraints and accommodate the anxieties.

Despite the multidimensional, interactive nature of the factors involved in the Lebanese conflict, it is necessary to separate them for the purposes of analysis and description. This section is intended to place the Lebanese conflict in the context of some of the principal components of the conflict vortex. Consequently, we shall consider four different elements — the identity conflict and the minority problem, the Lebanese political system, the regional conflict and the security problem, and the question of sovereignty. These four issues are central to Lebanon's situation today, and it is at least arguable that, broadly defined, they are the primary components of conflict in Lebanon. Although discussed individually for analytical purposes and clarity here, the four are highly interactive, and this interaction will become apparent in the next section.

2

Identity Conflict and the
Problem of Minorities

Political scientists and historians date the modern state system from 1648, the Peace of Westphalia, and describe it as a "system of nation-states." The concept of the nation-state is relatively straightforward – a modern state is composed of a single people or nation united by culture and history that identifies with the state as the essence and symbol of the nation. Although the nation-state is seen as the dominant form of political organization in modern history, in fact true nation-states are exceedingly rare, and the superpowers are in many ways the antitheses of nation-states, both the United States and the Soviet Union containing several distinct ethnic, religious, linguistic, and cultural communities. Of the approximately 150 sovereign states active today, perhaps a dozen could legitimately be called nation-states.

National minorities and their concerns have created major problems for the modern state form that collects ultimate and decisive power at the center. When the real power of the government is weak, it poses no threat to these communities. As real (rather than nominal) central government power grows, however, it may mobilize minorities who fear the loss of their autonomy and identity. Ironically, a strong central government may be the best source of protection for minority communities in multicommunal states. Constant fragmentation of the political order provides fewer assurances that basic needs will be met than does aggregation in a cooperative setting. The challenge, clearly, is to address perception and reality with equal sensitivity.

We are not writing the obituary of the multinational state. On the contrary, such states are the rule, not the exception. Multicommunal states have survived and indeed can flourish. At the same time, the technological revolution has not been kind to multicommunal states in which the aggregate identities of the communities have not already congealed around the state. As technology has enhanced the perception of the threat to community identity posed by central governments' new communication and transportation capabilities, so too has that technology provided more effective means to mobilize the communities whose identity appears to be threatened. Moreover, multicommunal societies provide ready-made arenas for external powers to extend themselves and to exploit the minority communities' fears in order to play a role inside the multicommunal state. At times, foreigners are actively recruited by minorities who try to manipulate the situation to "win" in the communal power game.

These issues, which may appear abstract, relate directly to Lebanon. Lebanon is a young state, but its identity is ancient. The Bible refers to Lebanon by name dozens of times and to its cities and other attributes still more frequently. Lebanon has enjoyed a crossroads culture from Phoenician times to the present day. Over the centuries, migrations to and from Lebanon have created a unique heritage at once undeniably part of and yet just as undeniably distinct from the surrounding area. The past decade of violence is at least in part a result of the traditions and complexity of the country and the heritage of its people.

A central debate in Lebanon's contemporary history has revolved about the country's identity. Division within Lebanon began in 1920 on the question of whether Lebanon was an Arab state artificially severed from the Arab world to which it must eventually return or whether Lebanon's independence from other Arab states reflected special and enduring historical circumstances that made the country unique. This historic question was especially powerful during the French mandate and the early years of independence, when the Muslim Sunni community in particular felt it had been artificially and unjustifiably separated from the great Sunni majority in Syria and the Arab world. By contrast, Christians, especially Maronites, were adamant about the distinctness of Lebanon and the finality of its independence. Two other minorities, Lebanon's Druze and Shi'a populations, were ambivalent about or supportive of Lebanon's independence, recognizing they would enjoy the security of being minorities among minorities in Lebanon rather than being small minorities submerged in a vast Sunni majority in Syria.

Over the decades of Lebanese independence the issue evolved, receding from the existential question of a sovereign Lebanon, for other states proved no more eager than Lebanon to relinquish their separate sovereignties in favor of a single Arab nation-state. Indeed, it is ironic but accurate to observe that the extreme forms of Arab nationalism and Nasserist pan-Arabism thrived in Lebanon well after they became outmoded elsewhere. No longer, however, did the bulk of the Lebanese Sunni community propose the abnegation of Lebanese sovereignty. Instead, by the 1970s and 1980s, the issue had become one of symbolic identity, cultural distinctness, and political autonomy.

Manifestly, the identity problem is deeply rooted in the composite soil of other issues. Identity conflict is intimately associated with sectarianism, confessionalism, ethnicity, the locus of nationalism, and Lebanon's crossroads heritage. The unresolved conflict over the preeminence of individual loyalties (or identity) is what links these phenomena. Too frequently have observers concluded that some Lebanese are "Christians first, Lebanese second," "pragmatic merchants first, ideological purists second," "Arabs first, Lebanese second," and so forth. Such contradictory observations cannot all be right—or can they?

The problem for Lebanon – and, incidentally, for most Third World countries – is not that this or that loyalty precedes loyalty to the state. Rather, it is that loyalties and identities are confused. Today's Arab nationalist may be tomorrow's Maronite; today's secular socialist may be tomorrow's Shi'a cleric. Indeed – and many contemporary examples commend themselves – today's Arab nationalist may be today's Maronite.

Primordial loyalties in Lebanon tend to create multiple streams of decision logics for each of the key individuals involved. How was one to know whether the late Kamal Junblat was speaking as a Lebanese, a Muslim, a Druze, a socialist, a party leader, or leader of the Lebanese National Movement? Whether Camille Chamoun was speaking as a Lebanese, a Christian leader, a Maronite, a party leader, or the head of the Lebanese Front? These examples are not at all atypical of the multiplicity of associations characteristic of the Lebanese.

Identity as a Defense Mechanism

Religious affiliation remains the single most important identity among the Lebanese. Moreover, its importance may be increasing rather than diminishing. The explanation for both these facts is that although an individual has many identities, those perceived to be threatened tend to increase in salience.

The Christians of Lebanon have long expressed feelings of insecurity about their status. Historically, this insecurity has focused on the surrounding Sunni world and the close links of the Lebanese Sunni community to coreligionists in Syria and other Arab Muslim states. A contemporary manifestation is the demographic fear of being engulfed within Lebanon, a concern that is more directly related to the Shi'a community, with its very high birthrate, than to the Sunnis, whose fertility rate is believed to be similar to that of the Christians.

Over the years the Lebanese Christian community has been divided on the preferred means of responding to what is perceived as the threat to their survival. All Christians, regardless of sect or location, have been socialized by a process that recalls earlier massacres of and discriminatory treatment toward Christians and that underscores elements of discriminatory dogma in Islam as well. Faced with the continuing crisis of survival, however, two approaches have dominated Christian thought: resistance and accommodation. The Maronites closely associated themselves with resistance. Concentrated predominantly in defensible Mount Lebanon (to which they had repaired as a result of persecution), they have been able to preserve their separate status through resistance. By contrast, the Lebanese Greek Orthodox, whose coreligionists are scattered throughout the Arab world, believe the survival of their community could best be ensured by a variety of means of accommodation, including strong support for secular politics. The Greek Orthodox have been at the forefront of secular political movements such as Arab nationalism, Ba'thism, and communism throughout the Arab world. Two Orthodox Palestinians, George Habash and Wadi Haddad — no relation to the author — founded the Arab Nationalist Movement while in Lebanon. Michel Aflaq, one of the two founders of the Ba'th Party is a Greek Orthodox. The Lebanese Communist Party is also headed by a Greek Orthodox. The third largest Christian sect in Lebanon after the Maronites and the Greek Orthodox, the Greek Catholic, tends to divide between these two philosophies. Isolated groups of Greek Catholics are often somewhat more accommodationist, while those in the Christian heartland frequently tend toward resistance, but the community has been far less active or visible than either of the other two.

No more secure have been the Druze, a small minority in contemporary Lebanon. Despite a few sanguinary episodes of violence, Maronite-Druze relations over the centuries formed the core of modern Lebanon, and Christian-Druze economic relationships are central to the Shouf, the Druze heartland. For centuries the Druze ruled much of what is today Lebanon, a much larger area than the Shouf itself. The continual decline of their area of predominance and their influence in modern Lebanon has been a source of deep concern and insecurity for the Druze community, which fears for its survival.

Nor have Lebanon's Shi'a felt secure. Cut off from the largest agglomeration of their coreligionists in distant Iran and Iraq, subordinated as Muslims in Lebanon by the Sunnis, and lagging behind all other communities in political and social mobilization, Lebanese Shi'a feel they have suffered the effects of severe discrimination by the Lebanese government. The Beqaa Valley and the south, where most of Lebanon's Shi'a have traditionally resided, were the least developed regions of Lebanon. Fractious relations with the Sunnis and especially with the Druze meant the Shi'a received little support from anyone. The strong Lebanese nationalism of a people that has traditionally seen its ability to realize communal objectives only through the Lebanese state has not led to a viable alliance with the Christians and has often placed them at odds with fellow Muslims.

The only major group displaying a sense of security in Lebanon has been the Sunni community – ironically, the weakest of the major sects in the country today. Lebanese Sunnis have traditionally maintained close ties to the Arab world, especially to Syria, and their security derives from their identity with this vast Sunni "sea" beyond Lebanon. Despite the ebb and flow of politics, the enveloping Sunni world will ultimately protect them. Until very recently Sunni leaders have tended to take for granted their right to leadership of the Muslim community as a whole, including both Druze and Shi'a.

The political implications of the role of sectarian identity as a defense mechanism in Lebanon have been far-reaching. The channeling of competition and friction into confessional identity – competition and friction that might otherwise have been dissipated in conditions of less structured reinforcement to religious identity – has created a confrontational setting for Lebanon's most basic component groups. Such a setting is a zero-sum game, in which any gain for one is perceived as a loss to the others, and increased security for one group is therefore an increased threat to others. What is lacking is an equilibrium of power for deterrence and mutual, balanced gain. In the present circumstances, only communal cohesion and the strength of one's community provide individual security. This fact explains more than any other the use of private militias, the durability of patron-client relationships, and the cynical and destructive nature of alliances in Lebanon.

Identity as a Conflict Mechanism

The question of identity of either a person or a group is a conflict mechanism – it gives meaning to events, types groups and persons, and perpetuates conflicts and the interests of parties to the conflict. Parties to protracted conflict situations tend to distrust each other's intentions and to engage in cycles of violence and destruction. Deception becomes the norm – and not merely deception of the opponent. What is even more striking is the degree to which deception of one's own group becomes the norm. Each thinks the actions of the other are tactical, solely intended to play for time to allow one to improve one's position.

In very general terms, many Lebanese Muslims believe their Christian countrymen to be unauthentic Arabs because they do not articulate their support for Arab nationalism in the same way Muslims do and because they raise questions about the wisdom of Arab policy with respect to matters of regional war and peace. Even when a Christian leader or a small faction voice sincere objection to the logic of a perpetual armed struggle with Israel, their attitude is automatically taken to be motivated more by communal identity than by personal and political preference. No more reasonable is the Christian view that questions the loyalty to Lebanon of Muslims who defend and subscribe to certain policies and ideas regarding Arab unity and the role of Islam. If a non-Lebanese Muslim such as Libyan leader Mu'ammar Qadhafi argues that Christian Lebanese must convert to Islam in order to live in peace in the region, it is automatically assumed by many Christians that all Muslim Lebanese must share the same view. No matter how vocally Christians and Muslims protest their adherence to Lebanon and to what it stands for, all public and private postures are filtered through systematic distrust and distorted to fit the basic and perverted premises of mutual perception.

For many and varied historical, social, and economic reasons, the major Lebanese communities find themselves in a situation in which no single religious community – and, increasingly, in which no social class – trusts the other beyond certain minimal levels, especially when it comes to issues of national destiny and policy. The lack of trust forces groups to redefine their objectives in very demanding terms and increases their rigidity. When one consistently attributes bad faith to the other side, opportunities for new learning patterns and breakthroughs for conflict reduction are minimized. When parties stop fighting and offer to talk, they are believed to be seeking a respite from war only to prepare for the next round. In other words, abnegation of conflict at the national level is not taken as an opportunity to reassess or a window to negotiate and build mutual confidence. Instead it is perceived as yet another occasion to prepare, stockpile, and work toward a "win." As a result, all sides continue to expect the worst of each other, and no matter how carefully formal ceasefires are proposed, or plans to move from war to peace are designed, no one takes them seriously.

One of the harshest costs of identity as a conflict mechanism is that it hides and to some extent changes the nature of competition for power common to any democracy, transforming it into a communal struggle. Thus, in Lebanon, the struggle for authority between the president and the prime minister, a struggle common to many political systems, is widely perceived as a Christian-Muslim struggle. In the same manner, the appointment to specific positions raises the specter of sectarian hegemony, the same process that in most states is not seen in sectarian terms. The sectarian coloration given to these processes in Lebanon reinforce fears, distrust, and antagonisms, focusing the negative feelings into a single channel. Part of the reason for this phenomenon may be found in the memory that Lebanese minorities retain from the days of the Ottoman Empire (which the Christians believe relegated them to second class status) or the French mandate (which the Muslims believe introduced Christian domination). At least as important a factor, however, has been the cynical manipulation of religious symbols by leaders to advance their own fortunes in the intricate and high-stakes game of Lebanese politics.

The Matrix of Community Views

Before considering the range of views in Lebanon's communities, several observations are in order concerning the representation and representativeness of these attitudes. Lebanon's sectarian communities are anything but internally homogeneous in their beliefs and interests. Moreover, political views (except on some issues of personal status) do not derive from religious dogma through a process of thorough, systematic review, assessment, and decision related to religious teachings or even from the political implications of such dogma. Indeed, there are no public opinion data to indicate the views of the communities, much less evidence to suggest a consensus. Community political positions in Lebanon are established within boundaries determined by leadership elites.

Lebanese political culture has permitted, in fact, encouraged, these elites to arrogate to themselves the sole right to determine these positions and to shift tactically where necessary.

This may be a useful time to suggest that the view that political change may bring violence is unduly limited. Conflict also engenders pressures for further change. It is very clear that one of the processes loosed by the conflict in Lebanon is an erosion of control by elites – not only traditional elites. Some writers have pointed to the rise of new social forces and new leadership elites – for example, Amal in the Shi'a community. The same processes of change and continuing conflict that propelled these new groups simultaneously reduced the power of tradition that had produced earlier elites – without substituting new forces of cohesion and legitimacy. The consequences are that new elites do not have the same control over their constituencies as their predecessors had over theirs and that all leaders lack legitimacy to mobilize and "deliver" their communities. The range of attitudes within communities is as great as ever, but the ability of leaders to establish limits has eroded.

The views within the Christian community operate on three dimensions: Lebanese nationalism, ethnicity, and sectarianism. In practice, given the identity issue already discussed, the Lebanese nationalist dimension is often (but not always) a function of the other two. In any event, the concepts surrounding the Lebanese nation are so divergent as to make it difficult to demonstrate the dimensionality graphically. By contrast, the other two dimensions can be displayed rather easily. In the schematic diagram, for example,

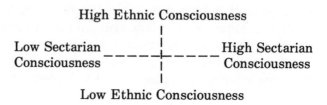

Christian views may be high in ethnic (Arab) content, low in sectarian (Christian), or the reverse, high in both, or low in both – and, of course, most should fall somewhere within the extremes. There are four principal schools of thought in the Christian community, each holding a range of views, but each at a distinct point in the matrix.

Highest in sectarian consciousness and lowest in ethnic consciousness are groups such as the Guardians of the Cedar. Their political views relate almost exclusively to the predominant position they ascribe to internal sectarian issues. Moreover, they do not identify with the Arab world, seeing in Lebanon a nation as well as a state. At the opposite point in the matrix are secularists who apotheosize Arab unity and Arab nationalism, permit these values to determine their political views, and disregard or condemn sectarianism. The Syrian Social National Party (SSNP), whose leadership is predominantly Greek Orthodox, has epitomized such views. In their own way, both of these groups represent the outside extremes of Christian thinking. Much more characteristic are two other groups.

The largest part of mainstream Christian political thinking has been the cluster of groups that acknowledges Lebanon's Arab character but also recognizes the salience of sectarian identity in Lebanon. These groups include Chamoun's National Liberal Party and the Kata'ib (Phalange) Party of the Gemayals', among others. Close to this position but quite distinct is that represented by former President Suleiman Franjieh, who puts equal weight on sectarian identity internally but much greater emphasis on Lebanon's Arab character. Indeed, a subtle but significant distinction between this view and the other Christian mainstream ideas is the assertion that the Lebanese people (not just Lebanon) are Arab. This position contradicts the argument of some Christian Lebanese that they are not Arabs.

The bulk of the Christian community, surrounded by Muslims and socialized in the history of religious identity and persecution, has long insisted on structural guarantees and behavioral indicators as an essential adjunct to the multiconfessional state. The National Pact of 1943 met these needs in ways not unlike the U.S. Constitution met the identity and security needs of small states in the late eighteenth century — by providing guarantees through the allocation of political powers to the affected identity groups.

Some Christian politicians have treated the National Pact as holy writ, refusing to consider modification, apparently in the belief that any changes, however minor, will lead ultimately to fundamental changes that remove the guarantees of security inherent in the pact's provisions. Others have supported change, but always with the continued insistence that all parties recognize and accept the need for guarantees to ensure Christian security. The range of views of those accepting modification is wide, some willing to consider only minor alterations (such as the numbers and relative communal representation in the Parliament), while others insist on much more far-reaching change, such as complete secularization.

Although it is unsafe to generalize about such diverse attitudes, once again the views tend to represent the dual dimensions discussed above. Secular groups (such as the Lebanese Communist Party and the Syrian Social National Party) demand an end to the confessional political system discussed below and a complete and total secularization of Lebanese politics. At the same time, the Arab nationalists among them advocate a much more active role for Lebanon in the Arab coalition against Israel than do the others.

Mainstream Christian groups are more restrained about change. They approve the principle of constitutional reform and accept the idea of modifications that will leave guarantees in place. Most are willing — at least officially — to accept the concept of secularization; some insist on it if changes are to be significant. By secularization, however, they mean not only the abolition of the confessional appointment and representation system, but also the end of sectarian personal status, so that education, social affairs, and all other government services are provided on a secular basis.

Most Christian groups have seen an assured veto power as their guarantee against domestic Muslim domination. For this reason, they accept diminution of the Christian president's powers or the reduction of their parliamentary power on condition of reduced central government powers in general. Indeed, Christian leaders have made it clear they do not insist upon a Christian presidency under conditions of decentralization.

Although many Christian leaders speak in terms of a unified Muslim position for tactical purposes, the range of views in the Muslim community is as diverse as it is among Christians – perhaps more so. Increasingly, Muslim views can be seen in terms of the same set of dimensions in the diagram above, yet this is a relatively new development.

The three principal Lebanese Muslim communities – Sunni, Shi'a, and Druze – come from very different traditions and approach political issues with distinct and divergent sets of interests.

In modern Lebanon – the post-1920 Lebanon in its present boundaries – the Sunni community was traditionally seen as the leader and dominant element among the Muslims. Geographically divided into several areas of predominance – the 'Akkar, Iqlim al-Kharrub, and especially the three coastal cities of Tripoli, Beirut, and Sidon – the Sunnis had pronounced differences. Beirutis, many of them merchants, were cosmopolitan, pragmatic, middle class, and rather secular in behavior. Leading Beirut Sunni families intermarried with non-Lebanese Sunnis, especially from Syria. By contrast, the Tripoli Sunni community remained much more insular and more closely tied at the political grass roots level to Syria. The violence in Lebanon after 1975 cut the Sunni centers off from each other to a great extent and prevented the emergence of a Lebanese Sunni leadership representing a broad cross section of the community.

The Druze had been the dominant group in much of Lebanon in centuries past – the old Mt. Lebanon-Shouf area. By the twentieth century, their dominance was limited to the

Shouf and even there it was shrinking. Although only about 6 percent of Lebanon's population, the Druze nevertheless dominate key terrain that overlooks Beirut and links Syria and Lebanon. Moreover, they maintain close ties with their coreligionists in Israel and Syria. Although their community remained more cohesive than any of the others, Druze religious leaders have watched with consternation as the power of the community eroded.

By contrast with the Sunnis, the Shi'a community exercised relatively little power in years past. The Shi'a, however, have a high fertility rate and emigrate much less than other communities, though temporary emigration (especially to Africa) for commerce was extensive for some decades. Shi'a of the Beqaa Valley remain heavily influenced by tribal traditions, while those of the south have played a more active role in national politics. Predominant in these two areas, the Shi'a have also become a primary factor in Beirut. Israeli retaliatory air raids and hostilities in the south, as well as dual control by Israel and Syria of the south and the Beqaa Valley, respectively, have forced large numbers of Shi'a to the capital's southern suburbs. Today, there are probably more Shi'a in Greater Beirut than members of any other single sect. In recent years, the Shi'a have been politically mobilized by new leaders who have reduced the control and influence of traditional Shi'a leaders.

Historically, and currently, the perspectives of these three components of the Muslim community are anything but coterminous. The two-dimensional measure of identity, however, once again proves useful in the Muslim context. Beirut Sunnis tend to rank highest on ethnic identity as Arabs, lowest of the three on sectarian identity. (Sunnis from other areas would also rank high on the first dimension, but higher on the second as well.) The Druze rank highest and most cohesively on sectarian identity. Shi'a are also high on religious identity, but vary more widely, with followers of traditional leaders significantly less motivated by purely religious perspectives.

For all Muslim Lebanese there is no question as to their Arab ethnic identity. Sunnis place greater emphasis on Arabism because this factor grants them additional leverage in Lebanon – it tends to translate to the internal power equation the vast Sunni majority of the Arab world. The same factor inherently reduces the degree but not the kind of Druze and Shi'a ethnic identity, which is certainly quite Arab. (Nevertheless, it is psychologically easier for both to deal with coreligionists at odds with the Arab world – non-Arab Iranian Shi'a, in the one case, Israeli Druze, in the other – than it might be for the Sunnis.)

Both Sunni and Shi'a communities are experiencing pressures from fundamentalist groups. Among the Shi'a the process has had a pronounced and highly visible effect and is linked to several factors, notably the whole process of political mobilization, which is itself related to the Lebanese government's neglect of the Beqaa and the south; the disappearance in 1978 of the Shi'a leader Musa Sadr; the Iranian revolution, Iran's activist strategy, and the close ties of Lebanon's Shi'a community with Iran; and the Israeli occupation of the south after 1982. Sunni fundamentalism is more limited, being most evident in Tripoli where fundamentalist groups have served as a rallying point against encroachments by the growing Alawite community. Outside Tripoli, Sunni fundamentalism seems to reflect the growth in religious consciousness across the Arab world, but is constrained in Beirut by the very strong tradition there of commerce and interaction with the West.

Since 1982–1983, a small but growing and increasingly powerful segment of Muslim opinion has openly embraced the goal of an Islamic state. The proponents of such a state include both Sunni and Shi'a fundamentalists, many of whom are involved in movements such as the *Harakat al-Tawhid, Hizballah,* and *Harakat Amal al-Islamiyyah.* Indeed, some mainstream Muslim leaders have made ambiguous statements clearly intended to maintain their legitimacy in the face of growing fundamentalism, statements at least implying endorsement of the Islamic state concept. Although it might be convenient to attribute the rise of this trend to Israeli or Christian Lebanese excesses, it is important to note that it is prominent in the northern city of Tripoli and in the Syrian-controlled Beqaa, as well as in the south and southern Beirut. This trend poses some very fundamental questions about the viability of the most basic philosophies of the pluralist Lebanese tradition.

Druze political views have usually encompassed Lebanese nationalist and Arab nationalist viewpoints, and, while Druze leaders have chosen allies in other communities, Druze community awareness has always produced tacit agreement among Druze leaders on measures to protect community interests through autonomy and special status. The Druze have openly indicated that if Lebanon should have a Western face for the Christian community, the Shouf should also have a Druze face. Shi'a are also dispersed on all political sides. Shi'a are represented in virtually every political movement in Lebanon and are also the plurality in the army. Unlike the Druze, the breadth of Shi'a participation does not represent a community determination to survive any outcome; it is instead a function of lack of cohesion spawned by low political mobilization as a community.

The Sunnis have had a much more distinct and characteristic political leaning toward Arab nationalism. The divergence within the Sunni community has tended to be between those extreme Arab nationalists favoring the unity of Lebanon with the surrounding Arab world and those who have maintained that although Lebanon must preserve and promote its Arab identity it should nevertheless retain its sovereignty and autonomy either temporarily (until the Arab world was ready for unity) or indefinitely. What has distinguished the Sunni political trends from Shi'a, Druze, and the predominant Maronite attitudes has been the ambivalence about and weakness of the Lebanese component.

The Arab nationalist view has not been limited to Sunnis. Its adherents have included some Druze and some Shi'a, but also many Maronites and a significant proportion of Greek

Orthodox. Many Sunni Arab nationalists identified with the Arab world at least partly for subconscious sectarian reasons, while non-Sunni Arab nationalists identified with the movement as a secular trend. Thus, Sunni Arab nationalists were often active in Arab nationalist parties per se, while non-Sunni Arab nationalists joined ideological parties that propounded Arab nationalism as an adjunct to their raisons d'être. Despite these significant differences, many issues important to Lebanon tended to unite all Arab nationalists. Typical were Arab-Israeli, Palestinian-Israeli, and some Palestinian-Lebanese issues.

3

Lebanon's Political System: Issues of Modernization and Reform

There are historical, sociological, and political anteced-
ents for the Lebanese consensus that precipitated the formal
Constitution of Lebanon and the informal National Pact of
1943. Conceptually, Lebanon's intercommunal balance and
peace were expected to be reinforced through the principle
of power sharing and confessional distribution of political offices. The political system, it was thought, would be organized in such a way as to create a ruling political majority
composed of persons representing the various confessional
groups in the country. The state would be republican, constitutional, developmental, and protective of its pluralistic
potential. It would be part of the Middle East, but true to
its broader perspectives and interests.

From a strictly formal and constitutional point of view,
the system looks very innovative and even elegant. The values embedded in the legal framework are humanistic and universal. In addition to being a free, parliamentary, and con-
sociational democracy, Lebanon's political institutions called
for strict affirmative and open distribution of power. Contrary
to the portrait often painted, the Lebanese political system
legally requires checks and balances and permits no group
to win at the expense of the majority or, indeed, to "win" at
all over the long term without a broad base of accord. Govern-

mental power at the highest level of the executive branches —
the presidency and prime ministry — must be shared as it is
in the legislature, the major civil service bureaucracy, and
so on down the line.

Sharing power is itself a constitutional requirement of
the Lebanese political system. Of course, the meaning and
practice of power sharing have evolved over time. Lebanon's
structure is more like a confederation of power, but a com-
munity-based rather than a geographically based confederation. The president cannot sign a decree without the prime
minister's approval and that of the cabinet minister involved.

The Lebanese system was designed to make government
pragmatic and representative. It was made to assure the
various communities that their rights would be taken into
account. No community could be systematically excluded,
nor could one dominate. Thus, in the Lebanese Constitution,
freedom and human and communal rights are assured. The
1943 National Pact was intended to preserve the autonomy
of the different communities through a straightforward but
interlocking system of checks and balances. The system that
ensued after the historic intercommunal agreement worked
to contain radical shifts and abrupt changes of political practice and control.

The magnitude of violence and its frequency after the
mid-1960s have shown that no matter how appropriate and
responsive the system was designed to be, and indeed was
from a formal and legal point of view, it failed. The Lebanese
system, like the best constitutions, was derived through the
free give-and-take of political discussion and compromise. It
represented the interests and expectations of all communities. More, it embodied the principles of Lebanese pluralism,
the development of Lebanese democracy, and the aspirations
of Lebanese humanism. Where did this system go wrong? Let
us consider three theories.

The external factors that imposed themselves on Lebanon have placed burdens on the political system wholly un-
foreseen at the time it was created. Regional wars and the
mistrust and anxieties that have developed since Lebanese

independence have made it difficult for all the Lebanese communities to work actively together to adapt the structure and correct whatever deformities existed. External threats, dislocation of populations as a result of the Arab-Israeli war, inter-Arab competition, and the attempts to recruit Lebanon into one side or another have jeopardized issues of identity, nationhood, the economy, the bureaucracy, and the like. Lebanese institutions could not function in a smooth and pragmatic way when the country was confronted with violence and disruption.

It is remarkable, and ultimately tragic, that the Lebanese political system was expected by many effectively to carry on and carry out normal functions in a society and in a region ever more polarized, ever more turbulent, and ever more unstable. If Lebanon was the Arab world's most democratic state, most devoted to human rights and to pluralism, this stance and its success, even if limited, only seems to have made it a target for greater demands, greater criticism, and certainly far greater expectations on the part of all – Lebanese and foreigner alike. The Lebanese system could not respond to the challenges of the movement from mandate to independence while everyone in the region was utilizing the internal societal cleavages to play in the Lebanese internal political game. A good case can be made that the system was overtaxed by external and internal demands and actions. The Lebanese system might have worked if it had been able to insulate (not isolate) itself from the regional stresses and strains. From a different angle, the structure and composition of this system made it particularly vulnerable to foreign demands and, therefore, constituted a major reason the Palestinians, Syria, and Israel acted as they did in Lebanon.

A second and somewhat different theory is that Lebanese political institutions were actually misapplied, exploited, and perverted by those entrusted with making them work for the collective good: the system was never used properly. According to this explanation, the complex system of power distribution was transformed into processes and structures supporting special interests within each community.

As the Lebanese system evolved, communal rights became representational rights. Thus, if a specific office was to be filled by a Sunni, for instance, it became the prerogative of the Sunni leadership to clear the candidate for that office. Consequently, the patron-client system evolved into an arena for personal and family gain and exploitation of certain elites within each community at the expense of others within the same community. This process led to permanent exclusion of new generational and alternative leadership groups and hence to alienation and charges of corruption and nepotism.

The Lebanese political system was designed to establish the political framework and to define the administration to modernize the state. Instead, this framework became an end in itself and continued to dominate the debate and set both the boundaries for and the agenda of action in the entire country. Thus, administrative reform and modernization never took place (except incrementally during the Fu'ad Shihab period of the late 1950s and early 1960s). What had been intended as checks and balances evolved into confessional polarization. Even the routine argument between the prime minister and the president over jurisdictional issues became showdowns between Christian and Muslim or Maronite and Sunni power sharing. Ultimately, the struggle engendered the psychological baggage and identity dilemmas discussed above.

A third argument is that the Lebanese political system was basically never appropriate to the country's circumstances. Because the system was organized around an intercommunal sharing of power, it was doomed. The political system of Lebanon did not reflect the real social system. It was not prepared to accommodate change and therefore was inadequate. Some argue that the recognition and acceptance of confessionalism is inherently reactionary. Others argue that the system's blindness to Lebanese demographic realities is its principal shortcoming. While one group condemns what it considers the overcentralization of the 1943 formula that placed too much power in the hands of the national government and not enough in local hands, another is equally critical of the impotence of the central government and a de facto decentralization that stressed local rights of the various communities at the expense of the country as a whole. Almost all groups in Lebanon raise one complaint or another against the system, although few have been able to work out the deformities or suggest generally acceptable alternatives. It cannot be doubted that the political system, in protecting confessional autonomy, confessionalized politics and society to a far greater degree than ever intended. All issues came to be seen through confessional lenses. Worse, the importance of confessionalism was greatest in times of sectarian unrest, so that the system promoted, rather than reduced or managed, conflict and increased, rather than controlled, pressures on itself.

I raise the issue of the political system here because much of the venom and vigor of Lebanese political leaders has been devoted to the subject over the past several years, and, too, because much more time, effort, and negotiation will be expended in this direction. It is only fair to disclose my bias. A political system is a method, not an end in itself. It provides the means by which, the rules for which, and the guideline within which a people pursue their political destiny. The system should reflect the political culture; if it fails to do so it will perish. But it is the system that will pass, not the people. For all its faults, the Lebanese political system can accommodate, with modifications and through evolutionary processes, the needs of Lebanon. The system should by all means be changed, but it is the will of the people that must ultimately determine the nature of the state—or the survival of the state of Lebanon. If the Lebanese can rebuild trust, if their leaders can exhort the Lebanese to invest themselves in the idea and ideals of Lebanon, the political order, indeed a number of alternative formulas, could operate effectively. But political institutions and constitutional documents do not make a nation. Structures must not be confused with will. If the will is there, the institutions can be created or molded to accommodate the diverse needs of the Lebanese people.

4

The Arab-Israeli Problem
and Security

Apart from the latent Syrian perspective that Lebanon was in fact part of Syria, Lebanon met independence without the border conflicts endemic to the Third World. Lebanon's brief and inconsequential participation in the first Arab-Israeli war of 1948–1949 was a stabilizing act because it led to a de facto peace on the border dividing Israel from Lebanon. For almost two decades this border was quiet, and no Arab country came closer to meeting Israel's search for acceptance and security than did Lebanon. Despite its shared borders with Israel, Lebanon was never seen by its Arab brethren as a confrontation state.

In the early years, Lebanon's stance, which was an informal neutrality vis-à-vis Israel, was tolerated by the Arab world as were Lebanon's autonomy and uniqueness. Governments had little real control over their territory and even less capacity to interfere effectively in each other's affairs. As these circumstances changed with the passage of time so too did the toleration of Lebanon's positions both toward the Arab world and toward Israel. One thing that did not change over time, however, was the Lebanese unwillingness to develop a modern army strong enough to deter external intervention. Some felt it would cost too much and derided the "wasted" resources other regional states were pouring into their military forces. Other reasons were also advanced:

- Lebanon's neutrality was seen as the country's shield;
- Lebanon faced no external threat;
- A strong military would inevitably embroil Lebanon in regional disputes and would be seen as a threat by others;
- Such an army might become involved in politics or might even stage a coup, a prevalent pattern in the Arab world at the time.

The irony of all these arguments is bitter, indeed. The lack of an army that could maintain order and deter aggression has certainly ended in costing much, much more than any resources Lebanon could have invested in an army. Lebanon's neutrality did not prevent others from intervening in Lebanese affairs. The lack of a deterrent invited and created threats on all sides. A stronger military might have been able to deter other regional powers and thereby prevent Lebanon's embroilment in regional disputes; in the event, the absence of a deterrent allowed others to intervene directly, plunging Lebanon into regional disputes. And, finally, the army's intelligence branch was a principal factor in Lebanese politics for years, even without a large army establishment.

In the late 1950s, during the presidency of Fu'ad Shihab, Beirut took an ever-more-Arab posture. Yet the demands of the Arab world, the Palestinians, and many Lebanese pushed toward an even more committed posture. Moreover, Lebanon's weakness created a vacuum that pulled both Israel and Syria, willingly or otherwise, into the country. Syrian intervention in 1968 and 1969 aided the rapidly growing Palestinian guerrilla movement. The latter in turn began to carry out attacks on Israel, prompting Israeli retaliatory raids designed to punish the Palestinians, encourage the Lebanese government to exert stronger control over its territory, and respond to domestic Israeli political pressure. By 1969, the border was no longer peaceful or neutral.

Ironically, then, as other Arab countries placed new restrictions on the Palestinians, the Lebanese government came under ever greater Arab pressure to make concessions to a movement that was polarizing the Lebanese, undermining internal security, and provoking foreign intervention. To non-Lebanese Arabs, Palestinian and others alike, Lebanon's weakness invited this hypocritical and short-sighted position. The Cairo Agreement of 1969 (and the 1973 Melkart Protocol) took Lebanon far from the neutrality that had insulated the country from a conflict involving forces far more powerful than those available to protect the Lebanese.

Insulation from the Arab-Israeli conflict had been seen as an expedient way to escape its costs: an arms race, punishing and tragic wars, economic dislocation, and social turmoil. Another important advantage of this insulation little appreciated at the time was that it gave no pretext to either of Lebanon's more powerful neighbors to intervene directly in the affairs, or to cast covetous glances at the territory, of Lebanon. The erosion of this insulation invited the entry of Syrian and Israeli power, in surrogate or overt form. Once in, neither has shown any eagerness to return to the status quo ante, nor can they, for the presence of each is seen as a threat to and therefore a rationale by the other.

The progression of intervention by Lebanon's neighbors has been spasmodic, but — and this is the suggestive portrait of the present and ominous portent of the future for Lebanon — both Israel and Syria have consistently created precedents, reinforced them, and then expanded them. The present and future behavior of each in Lebanon is now justified as a function of its own security requirements and its enemy's behavior, without reference to Lebanon or anything approximating the traditional rights attaching to national sovereignty. Israel's "right" to overfly Lebanese airspace is in fact less contested than Lebanon's right to deploy its own forces, composed and structured as it sees fit, anywhere on its own territory. The "right" to determine which concessions made to Israel compromise Lebanese sovereignty is arrogated to Syria, not Lebanon.

For the present, then, no one can any longer accurately

describe Lebanon as neutral. Strangely, Lebanon has become an active participant in the Arab-Israeli conflict not in the sense of being the ally of one or the other sides as much as it has become the terrain in which the war is fought. Over the course of a decade, Lebanon has become the only acceptable ground for overt Arab-Israeli hostilities. As long as the violence is contained in Lebanon, and especially if it is camouflaged in Lebanese clothes, the international community accepts it.

5

Sovereignty and External Intervention

Sovereignty is both a legal status and a real quality. The legal sovereignty of Lebanon has been unquestioned since independence. It is instructive to note, however, that the concept of sovereignty derives not from international status but from the degree of internal control exercised. Thus, "sovereignty" originally described states whose control over their territory was paramount.

The Lebanese state has not enjoyed sovereign rights over all of Lebanon since the late 1960s. Although real government control has varied in extent, it has rarely passed beyond the confines of the presidential palace and parts of Beirut in recent years. Other parts of Lebanon have been controlled by a variety of de facto "sovereigns" – the Palestine Liberation Organization (PLO), Amal, Syria, Sa'ad Haddad, Israel, a coalition of Christian militias, known as the Lebanese Forces, the Marada (the militia of Ex-President Franjieh), Iran, Libya, Palestinian guerrilla groups below the PLO level, and a multitude of small militias.

The problem of the loss of Lebanon's sovereignty should not be artificially distinguished from the previous subjects – of Lebanese identity, the Arab-Israeli conflict, and indeed even the Lebanese political system. I have attempted to lay some of the historical groundwork for a discussion of the sovereignty issue in the context of my treatment of these problems. Nevertheless, the sovereignty question is of critical importance and must also be addressed on its own merits.

Lebanon's physical sovereignty was largely coterminous with its boundaries from independence until the 1960s. Despite early Syrian ambivalence about the concept of an independent Lebanese state, none formally challenged Lebanon's credentials as such. The country was admitted to the Arab League, the United Nations, and other international bodies and maintained a visible regional and international profile befitting its role as Middle East entrepôt.

The fact that Lebanon's physical sovereignty was largely unchallenged is somewhat misleading, however. From the inception of the state, the Arab world has acted as if Lebanon's legitimacy were also an Arab issue. In some respects, virtually all members of the Arab League must deal with the conflicts between Arab nationalism and "local," "regional," or state nationalism. Lebanon's case has been complicated by its multiconfessional composition and especially by the prominence of the Christian community – which have undoubtedly created serious misgivings in some Arab lands – by the legacy of Lebanon's close ties to the West, and by its cosmopolitan perspectives, which frequently conflict with purely "Arab" views and dispositions. For these and other reasons, Lebanon has been subject to extensive demands to prove itself and by the scrutiny of its behavior by other Arab governments. Provocative appeals to the Lebanese in the name of Arab unity, Islam, or other similar rallying points have been directed to the Lebanese from outside. Despite this history – and all Arab governments, even those with the most "Arab," most Islamic, or most "progressive" credentials, have also been subjected to such appeals – at least Lebanon's physical sovereignty remained intact for some time.

The initial threat to and indeed victory over Lebanon's physical sovereignty derived from the Arab-Israeli conflict, specifically from the exile of the Palestinians. More than 150 thousand Palestinian refugees entered Lebanon as a result of the first Arab-Israeli war in 1948–1949. These Palestinians and their descendants have lived there as long as 35 years. For much of that time, virtually all Lebanese supported both the Palestinians' view and their cause in general.

The growing militancy of the Palestinian movement, especially after the June 1967 war, created new problems. Additional refugees and an arming process superimposed themselves on the Palestinian population in Lebanon – concentrated populations living near major urban areas and lines of communications. One of the legacies of the period of emergence of a militant Palestinian movement after 1967 was the launching of raids from Arab countries into Israel. Such raids had been a reality before 1967, but not from Lebanon. Predictably, Palestinian raids led to Israeli reprisals.

The Palestinian raids were only one facet of the threat to Lebanese sovereignty. The concentration, the arming, and the raids of the Palestinians in Lebanon and Jordan, and to some extent the raids from Syria, provoked not only an Israeli response but also domestic concern about the growing strength of the Palestinians as a domestic fact. In Syria, then-Defense Minister Hafiz al-Assad resolved the problem by placing the Palestinian fighters under strict military control. Jordan, despite the cost, had the wherewithal to crack down on the Palestinians. Lebanon, much weaker – ironically partly because the Lebanese thought that their smaller military forces would pose no threat to others and therefore avert conflict for themselves – could confront the Palestinians only at its peril, particularly in view of the country's communal divisions.

From the Palestinian point of view, Lebanon's sovereignty was increasingly seen as a price that had to be paid for the Palestinian cause. That is, while most Palestinians were too absorbed in the process of Palestinian mobilization or simply trying to exist to ponder the consequences of their rise in power for Lebanon, many did recognize the conflict between what they perceived as Palestinian rights (the right to carry out the armed struggle from whatever staging area was available) and Lebanese rights (the right to control national territory). In this conflict, however, they asserted the primacy of the Palestinian right – some because it was more immediate, some because it was more tangible, some because it was more "Arab," most because it was simply theirs.

The Palestinians then launched the first overt threat to Lebanese sovereignty. Israeli raids constituted an implicit second challenge. Ultimately, the meaning of the range and violence of Israel's attacks was, at the very least, that Israeli security made certain demands on Lebanon and that Israel's security borders extended well to the north of the armistice line that constituted the "international border." The invasion of 1978 and continuing support to Major Sa'ad Haddad militia (as well as to others) after that time gave substance to the concept.

But Syria, too, became even more ambivalent about the issue of Lebanon's sovereignty. From 1969 until the Syrian Army entered in June 1976, the Syrian government intervened in Lebanon indirectly through Sa'iqa, the pro-Syrian Palestinian guerilla group and through political and economic support to various factions. Although the 1976 Syrian Army entry into Lebanon was welcomed by the Lebanese government and subsequently authorized by the Arab League, the duration and role of the Syrian Army in Lebanon have also taken on a life of their own. Here, too, it is apparent – and indeed Syrian leaders have stated explicitly – that vital Syrian interests are at stake in Lebanon and that these interests, rather than Lebanese sovereignty, dictate their presence in Lebanon.

It is quite clear that powerful states generally delimit the boundaries of their vital interests beyond their international borders and therefore inside the territory of others. Such definitions usually do not, but sometimes may, entail or engender military excursions. Geographic boundaries are rarely if ever coterminous with psychosocial borders, security frontiers, or political and economic interests. What sets the Lebanese case apart is the regularity of foreign intrusion, the diversity of foreign interlopers, the breadth of intervention across political, social, economic, and military domains, the continuity of foreign physical control of the national territory, and the openness with which Lebanese nationals accept the intervention of various non-Lebanese in Lebanon.

The erosion of Lebanon's sovereignty is an insidious reality and is a function of the interaction of time, social change, and existential pressures. The state's legitimacy loses meaning when operational authority and control remain in the hands of others over long periods of time—when citizens must look to others to meet their most basic needs. National unity, another component of sovereignty, is seriously weakened when different segments of the population must look to different foreign powers to meet those needs. Given the salience of the identity problem in Lebanon, the whole fabric of the pluralist society is rent by multiple external military controls and the passage of time. The daily erosion of Lebanon's national role makes the hopes for political reform and social development seem remote, especially when the state is not able to exercise even the routine function of ensuring security and services, and when the Lebanese become mainly concerned with their basic security and the rudimentary elements of living.

A portrait of Lebanese sovereignty in 1984 would show real government control only over the area around the presidential palace in Ba'abda and the Ministry of Defense near Yarze. Varying degrees of government influence are also felt throughout the Mt. Lebanon area (from East Beirut almost to Batrun) and in West Beirut. In the former, real control is shared with the Kata'ib Party and Lebanese Forces. Government control is even more tenuous in West Beirut southward to the Awwali River, where a multiplicity of armed groups, many supported by various external powers, exerts substantial influence on the course of events. The south remains under Israeli occupation. The north and most of the Beqaa are under Syrian control. Tripoli is governed by several militias, and Palestinians occupy certain northern territory as well. Palestinians and other armed groups are in the Beqaa.

II

The Process of Resolution

6

Introduction

Attempts to resolve the present conflict have varied in intensity, substance, and initiators. The intensity of effort — in action, comprehensiveness, and scope — has closely followed the intensity and degree of violence of the conflict. The substance of the attempt has been a function of the perception of the nature of the conflict, on which there was always disagreement. When more weight was given to the external factors (the Lebanese-Palestinian/Syrian/Israeli conflict), as the Christians have tended to do, resolution rested in attempts at restoring sovereignty and security. Conversely, when the accent was placed on internal factors (the Lebanese-Lebanese conflict), as the Muslims have tended to do, resolution attempts focused on internal *entente* (accord) and reform. It is natural, therefore, that the polarization over the nature of the conflict has extended to the mode of resolution. What comes first, security or reform? Christians have tended to resist dialogue on reform under duress. Their general attitude has been one of: "Let us stop fighting first and then we are willing to discuss reforms." On the other hand, the Muslims have tended to argue that the conflict is political and that, therefore, security cannot be achieved militarily but only through political action; only a political accord can result in a lasting peace. Later on, the same type of polarization was extended to the occupation issue. Although the Christians were arguing, "Let us get all foreigners out and then the Lebanese can agree on internal issues in no time," the Muslims were countering with: "Let us agree on reforms first and then our unity will help us liberate our country."

Both camps have looked for outside help and initiatives for many reasons: to counterbalance external intervention and aggression, to act as a catalyst for reconciliation, to exert pressure on the "other" party, or to interject enough input into the delicate internal balance of power to bring an end to an otherwise protracted and open-ended conflict. Since the first crisis of sovereignty in the mid-1960s, the process of resolution of the Lebanese conflict has been a series of initiatives and interventions: Egyptian, Syrian, Arab, Western (U.S., French, and Vatican), Israeli, multinational, and, once again, Syrian. For presentational purposes, this process is divided into ten phases on the basis of the various conflict resolution initiatives and the themes that predominated during certain periods. In some cases, the periods were clearly divided; in others, past failures or changing circumstances gave way to new themes or initiatives. Choice of these phases is necessarily subjective, but in most cases the new approach (or theme) or the new initiative is relatively distinct. Where a resolution initiative was characterized by a new theme, I have considered it a separate phase. Likewise, a major new initiative, even if based upon the same conceptual approach, is treated as a new phase. This decision reflects the fact that new themes and new initiatives in virtually all cases reflect either failures or changes in the situation—or both.

7

Phase I. Identity vs. Sovereignty: The Egyptian Initiative (1965–1974)

The emergence of the Palestinian resistance in Lebanon in 1965 created a dilemma for both the Lebanese people and the authorities. Support for the resistance was dictated by the Arab affiliation heightened by the pan-Arabism of Egyptian leader Gamal Abdel Nasser and by the belief in the justice of the Palestinian cause. But the price was high: Israeli reprisals and possible internal disequilibrium. After the Arab defeat in the 1967 war and the concentrated efforts of the PLO to build its own base in Lebanon, the dilemma became more pronounced. On the one hand, the resistance movement gained prestige and became a symbol of Arab self-respect and aspirations, and, consequently, supporting it became a test of the genuineness of Arab identity and commitment. On the other hand, the armed Palestinian presence and activities ran contrary to Lebanon's sovereignty and injected a destabilizing element into the delicate balance of power between the various communities. Moreover, the country became polarized: the Muslims and leftists welcomed the Palestinian resistance as a natural ally and demanded freedom of action for the Palestinian commandos, the fedayeen; the Christians felt threatened by the predominantly Muslim Palestinian armed presence and called for the curtailment of its activities. A public opinion poll taken in 1969 showed that

73 percent of the Muslims compared to 26 percent of the Christians expressed support for the PLO.[1] As to whether commandos should be allowed to operate from Lebanon, the responses were

	Muslims	Christians
Support	56%	12%
Support with reservation	35%	31%
Not support	6%	53%

The Lebanese authorities attempted to control the actions of the Palestinian resistance, which led to a series of clashes in 1968 and 1969 between the Lebanese Army and the Palestinian fighters. The Lebanese Left and the Muslim "street" demonstrated to denounce "the plot concocted by the army against the resistance." As widespread violent fighting broke out in October 1969, Syria accused Lebanon of trying to liquidate the Palestine resistance "in coordination with imperialist and Zionist plots." In reprisal, it closed its borders with Lebanon and allowed commandos coming from Syria to attack and occupy some Lebanese border towns.

In an attempt to resolve the crisis, the Lebanese government requested President Nasser's mediation on October 25, 1969, and on November 3 the Cairo Agreement was concluded between Lebanon and the PLO to accommodate Lebanese sovereignty and Palestinian-Arab interests. The agreement, however, gave the PLO a clear victory. Although it mentioned that "the Lebanese civil and military authorities continue to exercise their full authority and responsibility in all parts of Lebanese territory and under all circumstances," it recognized the right of the PLO to use Lebanese territory for commando activities (in coordination with the Lebanese Army), and to exercise full control over the Palestinian refugee camps. Moreover the agreement clearly dictated the Lebanese position vis-à-vis the Lebanese-Israeli conflict: "The two sides affirm that the Palestinian armed struggle contributes as much to the safeguard of Lebanon's interests as to those of the Palestinian Revolution and all the Arabs."

The Jordanian-Palestinian confrontation of September 1970 and the summer of 1971 eliminated the PLO as a military power in Jordan and brought to Lebanon many commandos who were disillusioned with the established regimes and radicalized by the conflict. The PLO started to expand its operations in Lebanon and established a state-like infrastructure – military, political, social, economic – within the camps and in the south, in violation of the Cairo Agreement. This brought numerous Israeli reprisals and led to tense Lebanese-Palestinian relations. The PLO, however, continued to expand its influence without taking the Lebanese state and its authority seriously, knowing well that no rerun of the Jordanian experience could occur because of Lebanese polarization over the PLO presence and its alliance with the Muslims and the Left. In May 1973, however, Lebanese-Palestinian relations deteriorated into violent clashes between the fedayeen and the Lebanese Army. Syria immediately sent in units of the Palestine Liberation Army (PLA), closed its border with Lebanon, and mounted a press campaign against the Lebanese leadership. The other Arab countries exerted heavy political pressure on the Lebanese government on behalf of the Palestinians. Consequently, the president of Lebanon had to declare that there would be no "Black May" (in reference to the "Black September" of 1970 in Jordan) and concede to a ceasefire and return of the fedayeen to earlier positions. The violence ended with the signing of an agreement, known as the "Melkart Protocol," which reaffirmed the principles of the Cairo Agreement. Relations remained extremely tense, however, and Syria kept its borders closed, thus inflicting serious losses on the Lebanese economy. Only after a major round of Arab mediation efforts and Lebanese promises did Syria reopen its borders in August 1973. The Arab-Israeli war of October 1973 overshadowed inter-Arab differences, and the relations with the PLO and Syria improved significantly, culminating in President Franjieh's speech before the UN in November 1974 in which he pleaded the Palestinian case.

Some basic political facts emerged from these events,

which had a great impact on the subsequent behavior of the different parties.

1. A relationship of mutual support for mutual benefit was forged between the Palestinian resistance and certain Lebanese Muslims and the Lebanese Left. During the crisis the Muslim prime minister resigned and the Sunni leadership used the occasion to demand more equitable participation in ruling the country.

2. The Christians lost hope that the government, and more specifically the army, would be able to control the PLO, establish Lebanese sovereignty, and provide security. Consequently, the Christian parties started training and equipping militias of their own. They felt threatened by the increase in Palestinian power, particularly when some Arab countries labeled the conflict in Christian-Muslim terms, and leaders such as Colonel Qadhafi stated that the Christians in Lebanon had one of two options: to convert to Islam or to hand over the government to the Muslims and submit to an Islamic-Arab rule.

3. The collision between Lebanese sovereignty and Palestinian interest was met by general Arab support for the Palestinians, as if sovereignty were defined one way for Lebanon and another way for the rest of the Arab world. In the other confrontation states commando action was either prohibited (Egypt), eliminated (Jordan), or strictly controlled (Syria). Lebanon would have had no problem with its sovereignty and identity if its relations with the Palestinians had been governed by the same May 4, 1969 decree issued by the then Syrian Minister of Defense Hafiz al-Assad that regulated Palestinian resistance action in Syria. It was ironic that the Arab world forced the task of assimilating the Palestinian resistance and providing it with a base of operations on the least qualified country: the Lebanese Army could not handle the Israeli reprisals and Lebanon's internal delicate equilibrium could not survive the shock of a massive influx of armed elements from the outside.

8

Phase II. *Entente* and Security: The Syrian Initiative (1975–1976)

Lebanese-Palestinian relations deteriorated significantly at the beginning of 1975 for three main reasons. First, the PLO continued its raids into Israel in violation of the Cairo Agreement and invited intensification of Israeli retaliatory raids on southern Lebanon. Presidents Franjieh and Assad met January 7, 1975 to explore means to "help Lebanon stop Israeli aggression and safeguard its territorial integrity," but no operational measures were agreed upon. Second, the PLO's infrastructure, which was meant to serve the resistance and the refugees, was interfering with the lives of Lebanese citizens. The Christian leadership was critical of the Palestinian infringement on Lebanese sovereignty and Kata'ib leader Pierre Gemayel repeatedly warned in January 1975 of the consequences of Palestinian transgressions. Even Kamal Junblat, an ally and defender of the PLO, later reflecting on this period, was critical of the Palestinian behavior:

> One must admit that the Palestinians themselves, by violating the Lebanese law and by carrying arms and functioning in a police role at the entrances to the capital, have facilitated the preparation and conception of the conspiracy. In certain cases Palestinian patrols used to arrest government employees and director generals to check their identification, and in other cases Lebanese

and foreign residents were kidnapped and imprisoned for ... weak reasons. ... These violations, taken lightly at first, became unbearable. ... Palestinians should have collaborated with the Lebanese authorities so that law-breakers who take refuge in the Palestinian camps cannot escape the law. ... Had there not been this degree of transgression or violation of law we would not have seen this level of outrage over the Palestinians in isolationist circles [meaning Christians].[2]

Third, the PLO became more involved in Lebanese political life, which made the Christians feel increasingly threatened and the Muslims confident about attaining their demands for reform and equity. Shaykh Hasan Khalid, the mufti of Lebanon, described this involvement candidly:

Previously, we used to resort to political pressure only, as the only means for reform and equity. Then the Palestinian cause emerged, and we found ourselves united with the Palestinians because together we form one ideology. We and the Palestinians are one in terms of Arab identity, religion, and nationalistic views.[3]

After the army clashed with PLO commandos in January 1975 and intervened in February to normalize the situation in Sidon following the fatal shooting of former Deputy Ma'rouf Sa'd, who was leading a demonstration against a newly formed fishing concern headed by Maronite leader Camille Chamoun, internal polarization surfaced. Strikes and demonstrations were staged against the intervention of the army in the Muslim areas, by the Left, and in support of army intervention in the Christian areas. Leaders of the Christian parties—the Kata'ib and the National Liberal Party—condemned the PLO's interference in Lebanon's internal affairs and called for a revision of the Cairo Agreement. Leaders of the Muslim community (Sa'ib Salam and Rashid Karami) and the Left (Kamal Junblat) accused the army of violating its proper mandate and called for a revision of the national defense law, which governs the organization and operations of the army, and an amendment of the communal representational distribution in the state.

Political Mediation and First Aid Treatment

Violent confrontation between the Palestinians and their Lebanese allies and the Christian militias was instigated by the famous April 13, 1975 incident of Ayn al-Rummaneh, a Christian suburb of Beirut, in which, according to the police report, Palestinian commandos opened fire on Kata'ib Party militia handling security during the inauguration of a church attended by Pierre Gemayel and killed the chief of the local militia and one other member. The Kata'ib militia retaliated by opening fire on a bus carrying Palestinians from Sabra to Tel al-Za'tar camp, in which 27 passengers were killed. Politically, internal polarization was intensified. The Christian community rallied behind the Kata'ib and the National Liberal Party and demanded the intervention of the army. The Lebanese leftist groups, followed by the "Arab Front Participating in the Palestinian Revolution," both headed by Junblat, called for a political and economic boycott of the Kata'ib Party. When the cabinet resigned and fighting spread throughout Beirut, President Franjieh formed a government of military officers on May 23, which was welcomed by the Kata'ib Party and the National Liberal Party and rejected by a Muslim summit in which PLO leader Yasir Arafat participated. In an attempt to deal with the militarily explosive confrontation and the political impasse, Syria commissioned its Foreign Minister 'Abd al-Halim Khaddam to resolve the situation, which marked the operational beginning of the Syrian initiative. This initiative quickly broadened in the reflection of regional events, as Egypt took its first step out of the Arab coalition against Israel by signing a second-stage disengagement agreement ("Sinai II") in September 1975. Syrian attitudes toward Lebanon and the PLO were dramatically affected by Sinai II.

The philosophy of the Syrian initiative was subsequently articulated by President Assad in a speech on July 20, 1976 at the Syrian University:

• Syria perceives the Lebanese conflict as the consequence of an imperialist plot to liquidate the Palestinian resistance, confuse Syria, and partition Lebanon.
• Syria is concerned with the Lebanese conflict because it considers Syria and Lebanon as one country and one people with common interests.
• Israel wants to partition Lebanon for political and ideological reasons: to nullify the concept of a secular democratic state and discredit Islam and Arabism.
• This conspiracy can only fulfill its objectives through fighting. So, to thwart the conspiracy, fighting should be stopped and a national accord established.

Consequently, for one full year, Syrian mediation and intervention concentrated on cease-fires, a balance of power to end the fighting, an internal *entente*, and control of the PLO.

The first act of the Syrian initiative was a round of mediation, interrupted by renewed fighting, which led to the formation of Prime Minister Rashid Karami's "government of national salvation" of July 1975 and to a cease-fire that held for two months.

The second act of mediation came after the resumption of fighting in August and September. This time security and reform were coupled with the hope of providing a political foundation for the cease-fire. So, when the cease-fire was announced on September 24, the creation of a Committee for National Dialogue was also announced. The 20 members represented the different communities and positions in an attempt to develop a program of political and social reform as a basis for national reconciliation. The committee devoted the first four sessions to questions of security, and during the fifth session it established three subcommittees for political reform, social issues, and economic and finance issues. The subcommittee on political reform was faced with the

Kata'ib Party's call for total secularization, which was rejected by the Muslims, and the Muslim's call for abolition
of confessional considerations in public office, which was rejected by the Christian parties and groups. The cabinet then
debated the issue on November 12 and 15, and asked the
president and prime minister to study the different proposals.
After a cabinet meeting on November 29, both president and
prime minister announced an imminent solution to the crisis:
national reconciliation, expansion of the cabinet, reforms, and
Lebanese-Palestinian negotiations. Although a brief cease-
fire was observed, national dialogue reached a deadlock because the various parties insisted on their own positions.

Syrian mediation entered into a third stage of stepped
up intervention. This time Syria did not leave the Lebanese
to sort out their own differences and formulate their program
of reform on their own. Instead, it acted as a catalyst and
as an initiator along two lines. First, it invited almost all the
prominent Lebanese leaders to Damascus for talks, including
Pierre Gemayel and a large Kata'ib Party delegation, in an
attempt to take the posture of a neutral mediator. This signal
to the Christian camp was immediately followed by the withdrawal of Sa'iqa and the pro-Syrian Ba'th party from the National Movement (the coalition of leftist parties headed by
Junblat). Second, Damascus proposed on December 26 a solution to the crisis in the form of a five-point plan: (1) equality
in the number of Christian and Muslim deputies in Parliament, (2) election of the prime minister by Parliament, (3)
establishment of an economic and social council, (4) abolition
of confessionalism in the civil service, and (5) adherence to
agreements concluded with the Palestinian resistance.

The Constitutional Document:
An Unfilled Prescription

The intensive Syrian effort did not bring about its objectives
of political *entente* and peace. Internal polarization, even on
the nature of the conflict, remained strong. President Fran-

jieh, expressing the Christian view, announced in the cabinet meeting of December 12, 1975 that the PLO did not respect its agreements with the government, while Prime Minister Karami, expressing the Muslim view, announced a few hours later, after meeting with Yasir Arafat, that the present crisis was purely Lebanese and that the Palestinian resistance had nothing to do with it. Moreover, a Maronite summit at the presidential palace and a Muslim summit at the mufti's residence, with Arafat's attendance, highlighted the differences. On the security side, fighting between the Christian militia and Palestinian-Leftist forces intensified. The Christian militias took over Muslim enclaves in their areas, captured the predominantly Christian Palestinian camp of Dbayah, and imposed a blockade on the Tel al-Za'tar camp. The Palestinians and leftist forces, along with Sai'qa, occupied and destroyed the two Christian towns of Jyeh and Damour. Moreover, a PLA brigade entered Lebanon from Syria, linked up with Palestinian and leftist forces, and advanced into the mountains overlooking Beirut. On January 21, 1976, a small group of about 1,000 from the Lebanese Army, under the command of Lieutenant Ahmad Khatib (a Sunni), mutinied and formed the Lebanese Arab Army, with headquarters in the Beqaa, in support of the Palestinian leftists.

On January 21, Syria renewed its mediation efforts. Foreign Minister Khaddam acted swiftly. The next day the president's office announced that the Syrian initiative had led to an agreement toward a comprehensive solution to the crisis, which provided for the creation of a joint Syrian-Palestinian-Lebanese military committee and the formulation of a set of basic principles for reform. Syria's intervention followed three lines: first, a cease-fire was reached and directly supervised by Syria through the tripartite committee; second, Khaddam declared that Syria guaranteed the implementation of the Cairo Agreement; and third, the Syrian delegation held discussions with Lebanese leaders on the substance of an overall political agreement, which was finalized between Presidents Franjieh and Assad on February 7. On February 14, President Franjieh announced, as a result of the Syrian mediation, a "constitutional document" representing a 17-point program of reform derived from the Syrian 5-point plan. The document, which became the basis for further dialogue in later years, affirmed Lebanon's Arab character and called for (1) the formalization of the tradition of distributing the three highest offices among the Maronites (the president), the Sunnis (the prime minister), and the Shi'a (the speaker of Parliament); (2) more equity in power-sharing by allocating equal seats in the Parliament to Christians and Muslims, election of the prime minister by the Parliament, and the formalization of the traditional powers of the prime minister; (3) the preparation of laws to make the president, prime minister, and ministers accountable; (4) the strengthening of administrative decentralization; (5) the abolition of confessionalism from the civil service with the exception of category 1 positions; (6) economic, social, and educational reforms; and (7) the affirmation of responsible freedom of the press. The implementation of this program was contingent upon the implementation of the Cairo Agreement.

This program of national action was a compromise among the demands of the parties to the conflict. The Christians were assured that no concessions would be made before security and sovereignty were achieved, and their guarantee of the presidency was reconfirmed. The Muslim and leftist demands for institutional reform and social justice were met. The Palestinian resistance's right to movement and action under the Cairo Agreement was reaffirmed. The program nonetheless was met with reserve by most of the warring parties. The Christians felt threatened because the document accepted the Palestinian armed presence and made them give major concessions to the Muslims. The Muslim leadership opposed the confessional designation of the high offices and were not satisfied with the powers of the prime minister, but declared they would accept the program as a "temporary arrangement." The Left was disappointed by the sectarian basis of the document and the granting of only "responsible" freedom to the press. The Palestinian resistance did not comment on the program but did not appreciate the Syrian posture.

PLO leader Abu Iyad stated on February 15 that "no regime
—be it reactionary, progressive, or otherwise—can impose its
tutelage on us."

The constitutional document, the climax of Syria's political initiative, was supposed to resolve Lebanon's crisis
(both the Lebanese-Palestinian and Lebanese-Lebanese dimensions), and put an end to the war and start a new era of
peace and reconstruction. The opposite took place: Lieutenant Khatib's Lebanese Arab Army supported by the Palestinians and Leftists, took over the army barracks in the
south, the north, and in the Beqaa, the Palestinian and Leftists Joint Forces launched a heavy two-pronged offensive in
downtown Beirut and the mountains, and in March 1976
Colonel Aziz Ahdab, after an inept military coup, called for
the resignation of the president, which was followed by similar calls from the Islamic Council and the Palestinian leadership. Syria continued its contacts with the Christian and
Muslim leadership but cut off its supplies of arms and am-
munition to the Palestinians and completely severed its relations with the Left.

A Revised Diagnosis

Why did this political phase of the Syrian initiative fail? Both
Presidents Assad and Franjieh reached the conclusion that
the treatment was based on a wrong diagnosis. The problem
was much more serious. Six months later, in September 1976,
President Franjieh, in his farewell speech, accused the Palestinians of conspiratorial objectives:

> Their first objective was to obtain gradually full control
> over Lebanon by installing certain kinds of puppet rul-
> ers who will be in harmony with the Palestinians, the
> actual rulers. However, another objective evolved while
> work on the first was going on. Their second objective
> was to establish a Palestinian homeland, a part of which
> will be in the south of Lebanon, of a size dependent on
> the magnitude of their victory over the Lebanese.

President Assad, in his speech of July 20, 1976, had questioned the motives of the Palestinian resistance and the Lebanese National Movement for continued fighting after Syria secured for them all they asked for. He accused them of

> misleading public opinion in the Arab world, and maybe the world, into thinking that they are defending the Palestinian resistance. The truth of the matter is that there are forces within Lebanon and in the international arena that wish to exploit the Palestinian resistance for their tactical or strategic objectives. The Palestinian resistance fights now for the objectives of others and against the interests and aims of the Palestinian people. . . . Every mask has fallen; so the issue is not what we used to say or be told; the issue is not between Right and Left, nor between progressive and reactionary, nor between Muslim and Christian; it is an issue of vengeance. . . .

These two conclusions point to an alliance of mutual benefit between the Lebanese Left and Muslim Right on one hand and the Palestinian resistance (Right and Left) on the other hand. Palestinian spokesmen did not treat this alliance as a secret:

> We are not neutral in the Lebanese conflict. The National Movement supported us and stood by us during the different crises, and our utmost duty is to stand by it and provide it with every material, military, and moral support.[4]
> The Palestinian revolution is in one bunker with the Lebanese National Movement. . . . We are a part of the Lebanese National Movement.[5]

The Palestinian Right, mainly the Fatah movement, saw in controlling Lebanon vast opportunities to improve its chances of liberating Palestine. First, the resistance movement could expand its base of operations and utilize the communication and political infrastructure of Lebanon. Second, it could acquire enough influence to exercise further political and military pressure. Third, Lebanon could be held hostage to be exchanged for the West Bank at the right time. The Palestinian Left was involved in the Lebanese conflict for ideological reasons. Both the Popular Front for the Liberation of Palestine (PFLP) and the Democratic Front for the Liberation of Palestine (DFLP) have their roots in the Arab Nationalist Movement, which believed that the liberation of Palestine required Arab unity and power, which in turn required a change in the political, social, and economic state of the Arab countries. Both Fronts called for the overthrow of traditional regimes and the establishment of revolutionary proletariat power. Consequently, the alliance of the Palestinian Left with the Lebanese Left-Muslim coalition was transitional in order to set up such a regime. Again the Palestinian leaders spoke freely of their intentions. Nayif Hawatmeh (head of the DFLP) defined the solution of the Palestinian problem in terms of a change in the balance of power in favor of the national liberation movements, and this "change cannot take place except by pushing the Arab nation to carry arms and wage a popular liberation war, not only on the Palestinian and occupied Arab border, but throughout the whole Arab territories."[6] George Habash, chief of the PFLP, was more specific: "The Palestinian resistance will not give up any of the rights it acquired in Lebanon. . . . We have another mission in Lebanon – and we are not ashamed to register it before you and the whole world – which is the support of the Lebanese gun that was raised by the proletariat, the oppressed, and the poor of Lebanon."[7] Meanwhile, the Lebanese Left admitted that it "tried to divert the conflict from Lebanese-Palestinian to Lebanese-Lebanese so as to prevent its Arabization or internationalization and to save the (Palestinian) resistance a lot of embarrassment."[8]

Military Intervention: A Surgical Procedure

When the Syrian political initiative failed, Syria intervened militarily in June 1976 with the proclaimed aim of preventing the Palestinian-leftist coalition from scoring a military victory, which would have led to partitioning of the country, foreign intervention, and negative consequences for the Palestinian and Arab cause. The Syrian intervention was welcomed by the Christian leadership and opposed politically and militarily by the Palestinians and Kamal Junblat's Lebanese National Movement. The Arab League, upon the request of the PLO, decided to send to Lebanon an Arab Peacekeeping Force to replace the Syrians. Understandably, this move was first opposed by the Christian leadership and was then accepted only after assurances were given that the force would not interfere with the Syrian initiative. Although the force was actually deployed in Beirut, the Syrian Army continued its offensive in the mountains and the south against the Palestinian-leftists, and the Christian militia took over the Palestinian camps in the eastern suburbs of Beirut. These events prompted an Arab mini-summit in Riyadh and an enlarged meeting in Cairo in October 1976.

9

Phase III. Deterrence and Identity: The Arab Initiative (1976–1982)

The Arab League made many attempts to mediate in the early stages of the Lebanese conflict through meetings of Arab foreign ministers and through special mediation missions by Secretary General Mahmud Riyadh and special envoy Hasan Sabri al-Khuli. Syria and its Lebanese allies – the Muslims and leftists first, then the Christians – kept opposing any Arab intervention. Only in June 1976 did Syria accept the principle of Arabization of the Lebanese conflict and attended the special meeting of the Arab foreign ministers in which the Arab Peacekeeping Force was established. The Arab initiative, however, was only made operational after the Riyadh and Cairo summits in October 1976.

Creation and Deployment of the ADF

The results of the Riyadh summit, endorsed by the Cairo summit, affirmed the "collective Arab role" and presented a comprehensive plan (with decisions, mechanisms, and schedule) to end the war in Lebanon and return the country to normalcy. The decisions focused on the three major elements of the crisis: (1) security – a cease-fire and definite halt to the fighting throughout all of Lebanon, (2) sovereignty – the ap-

56

plication of the Cairo Agreement, and (3) internal accord —
an invitation to all Lebanese parties to enter into a political
dialogue for achieving national reconciliation. The meeting
established two mechanisms to implement these decisions:
(1) an Arab Deterrent Force (ADF), under the command of
the president of Lebanon, to impose the cease-fire, apply the
Cairo Agreement, ensure collection of heavy arms, maintain
internal security, and assist the Lebanese authorities to reac-
tivate public services and state institutions and (2) a committee comprising the representatives of Saudi Arabia, Egypt,
Syria, and Kuwait to ensure, in coordination with the president of Lebanon, the application of the Cairo Agreement. The
reestablishment of peace, including the withdrawal of Palestinian armed forces from areas occupied since April 13, 1975,
was scheduled to take place within a period of 45 days.

The ADF was formed predominantly from Syrian troops
(80 percent), with symbolic contingents from Saudi Arabia,
Sudan, the United Arab Emirates (UAE), and South Yemen.
The ADF was accepted by the Lebanese National Movement
and lukewarmly accepted by the Lebanese Front — but only
after Jordanian mediation. The ADF was deployed throughout all of Lebanon except in the south, where it was deployed
only to the Litani River, which approximated Israel's "red
line." This deployment put an end to the fighting and led to
the formation of a broad-based apolitical government.

The "Lebanization" of the ADF

Peace, however, did not last long. Two developments derived
from the Arab-Israeli conflict spilled over into the Lebanese
scene, leading to a shift in Syria's alliances and consequently
a change in the perception and posture of the predominantly
Syrian ADF.

The first development was Egyptian President Anwar
Sadat's trip to Jerusalem in November 1977, which led Syria
to realign itself with the PLO and the ADF to become lenient
with the PLO in applying its part of the Cairo Agreement.

The PLO did step up its attacks on Israel in the south, which resulted in Israeli retaliation and, finally, an Israeli invasion in March 1978. The UN Security Council (Resolution 425) subsequently called for (1) "strict respect for the territorial integrity, sovereignty and political independence of Lebanon within its internationally recognized boundaries" and (2) withdrawal of Israeli forces from all Lebanese territory. It also decided to create the United Nation's Interim Force in Lebanon (UNIFIL) to restore peace and assist the government of Lebanon "in ensuring the return of its effective authority in the area." Subsequently the Israelis withdrew and UNIFIL has been deployed in the south.

The second development was the gradual break between the Christian camp and Syria over the issue of rapproachement between the Christian militias and Israel, especially after these militias and some units of the Lebanese army led by Major Sa'ad Haddad, supported by Israel, fought the Palestinians and their leftist allies and established a narrow enclave near the Israeli border. These developments were paralleled by the reestablishment of links between Syria and the Lebanese National Movement.

The Syrian realignment placed the ADF on a collision path with the Christian leadership and the state authorities. Clashes erupted between the Syrian contingents of the ADF and the Christian militias (and the Lebanese Army, at one point) and evolved into heavy fighting in which East Beirut and the Christian suburbs were heavily bombarded by the Syrians.

The Lebanese Parliament, in a unanimous decision on April 27, 1978, tried to reposition the ADF and other armed forces in Lebanon in accord with Lebanese sovereignty and Arab and international agreements. The parliamentary document reaffirmed (1) a commitment to the unity, sovereignty, and the territorial integrity of Lebanon, (2) the resolutions of the Riyadh and Cairo summits, (3) the Palestinian pledge to cooperate with the Lebanese authorities to bring the country back to normalcy, (4) UN Resolution 425, and (5) the terms of reference of the ADF. It called for respect for UN

Resolution 425, particularly regarding Lebanese sovereignty, the termination of Palestinian and non-Palestinian military operations from Lebanon, the prevention of any military presence except the forces of the legal authorities, the enforcement of Lebanese laws and regulations for all Lebanese and non-Lebanese residents without exception, and the adoption of developmental and economic policies that promote equal opportunities and social justice.

This united Lebanese position was quickly overtaken by renewed fighting between the ADF and the Lebanese Forces, which was marked by massive shelling and heavy casualties all through the summer and fall of 1978, and in Beirut, the Metn, and Kisrwan. The Maronite leadership accused Syria of wanting to exterminate the Christians, turn Lebanon into a confrontation state with Israel, and ultimately absorb Lebanon into a Greater Syria entity. The Syrians, on the other hand, accused the Kata'ib and the National Liberal Party of aligning themselves with Israel and working to partition Lebanon. They maintained that, therefore, they should be liquidated in order to preserve Lebanon's Arab character.

The magnitude of the conflict triggered wide external reaction. Israel's prime minister pledged not to abandon the Christians. President Jimmy Carter suggested, on September 28, a conference on Lebanon, under UN auspices, which would include all the Lebanese parties as well as Syria, Israel, Egypt, Saudi Arabia, the United States, and France. The idea failed because Syria rejected it as an attempt to impose U.S. tutelage. France, on October 3, then proposed a redeployment of the ADF and the creation of a buffer zone between the ADF and the Christian militias, manned by Lebanese army units composed of both Christians and Muslims and commanded by a joint Syrian-Lebanese committee. The proposal was supported by Washington and London but rejected by Damascus. On October 6, the UN Security Council unanimously adopted a resolution calling for a cease-fire "so that domestic peace and national reconciliation can be restored" and dispatched a special envoy to facilitate the implementation of the cease-fire.

The Re-Arabization of the ADF:
The Beiteddine Conference

President Ilyas Sarkis, fearful of the implications of the internationalization of the crisis, now turned to the Arab world to resolve the conflict. He visited Syria on October 6, to negotiate a halt to the shelling and then toured other Arab countries to secure their support for a conference to settle the conflict. The Beiteddine Conference was held on October 15, 1978 and attended by foreign ministers of the countries participating in and/or financially supporting the ADF. The conference studied the different dimensions of the conflict, especially the security side, and reached the conclusion that the conflict needed a comprehensive treatment based on a set of principles that would address the different components of the crisis (sovereignty, identity, the Arab-Israeli conflict, and reform) and meet the demands of the different parties to the conflict. The conference thus emphasized (1) Lebanon's unity, independence, sovereignty, and territorial integrity; the state's exercise of its authority over all Lebanese territory; and the termination of all armed manifestations coupled with the collection of arms and the banning of the carrying of arms; (2) Lebanon's Arab identity; (3) the enforcement of the law against those who dealt with the Israeli enemy and the condemnation of all forms of such dealings; and (4) work on reaching a national accord among the Lebanese parties to the conflict and on adopting reforms that would assist in strengthening national unity and eliminating causes of armed conflict. The conference also endorsed Syria's actions in Lebanon by calling for a full implementation of the Riyadh and Cairo summit resolutions, which implied a deployment of the ADF throughout Lebanon, and at the same time called for the rebuilding of the Lebanese Army "on balanced and national bases" (a Syrian demand) to replace the ADF (a Christian demand). Operationally, the conference formed an Arab Follow-up Committee composed of representatives from Saudi Arabia, Syria, and Kuwait to be at the disposal of President Sarkis.

The ADF Question:
To Withdraw or Not to Withdraw

The Beiteddine resolutions were endorsed by the Lebanese cabinet on October 21, 1978 and a detailed operational plan derived from them was developed. The results on the ground were mixed. Tensions eased as Syrian contingents were replaced by Saudi troops in some Christian areas and were accompanied by a Saudi diplomatic thrust aimed at making the Christians feel secure enough to break relations with Israel. Meanwhile, the Lebanese government drew up an overall security plan including the gradual replacement of the ADF by the Lebanese Army. But Syria, successively, put three conditions for the withdrawal of ADF: a revision of the structure of the Lebanese Army, settlement of the problem of the collaborators with Israel – mainly the Christian militia in the south – and, finally, national *entente*. In the process, non-Syrian troops withdrew from Lebanon, and, by early May 1979, the ADF became totally Syrian. The renewal of its mandate then became controversial internally and in the Arab League. Syria, however, fearful that the Arab League might not renew the ADF mission, developed an independent rationale for its presence in Lebanon, articulated by Foreign Minister Khaddam:

> It should be clear to everyone that when we entered Lebanon we did it for national considerations. Our presence or withdrawal from Lebanon is linked to these considerations and the Arab League is not involved in such a decision. . . . Our basic and principal demand is for Lebanon to be one and Arab, capable of doing its share and playing its role in the Arab-Israeli conflict.[9]

The first condition for the ADF's withdrawal was easily met by passing a new army law on March 13, 1979, which reflected the "balanced and national bases" demanded by Syria and its allies. The second condition was much harder to achieve. The Lebanese government considered Major Haddad a deserter, issued a warrant for his arrest, and decided to send regular army units to the south. Haddad, in response, proclaimed his enclave a "Free and Independent Lebanese" state on April 18 and prevented the Lebanese Army from entering. The PLO and the Lebanese National Movement strengthened their control over the rest of the south and prevented the deployment of the Lebanese Army there. The PLO stepped up its operations and, as a consequence, Israeli retaliatory raids increased.

Once more, Lebanon appealed to the Arab community for help. At the Tunis summit meeting of November 20, 1979, Lebanon called for a complete withdrawal of the Palestinians from the UNIFIL zone, a halt to shelling of Israel across Lebanon's borders, and a halt to PLO announcements from Beirut claiming credit for commando operations. The summit, however, under pressure from the PLO, supported a compromise enabling the Palestinians to keep their bases in southern Lebanon but pledging them to halt their operations against Israel temporarily. This position set the stage for a protracted conflict in the south, with a Palestinian presence, the continued existence of Major Haddad's Free Lebanon, and violent clashes between the Palestinians and their allies on one side and the Israelis and their allies on the other side. The problem was further complicated by the sudden withdrawal of the ADF from the Beirut-Sidon area in January 1980, accompanied by a Palestinian takeover, and an ADF threat to withdraw from Beirut in early February, provoking the possibility of renewed fighting. In response, the Lebanese cabinet requested that the Lebanese Army fill the vacuum created by the ADF withdrawal — a decision that, as usual, polarized the country. The Lebanese Front and the Islamic Coalition supported the cabinet decision, while the Lebanese National Movement rejected it and the Palestinians deplored it because it "ignored the legitimate presence of the Palestinians in Lebanon." Consequently, no withdrawals occurred.

The third condition, national *entente*, was the major platform of the cabinet of Prime Minister Salim al-Hoss. In February 1980 President Sarkis and Prime Minister Hoss held a series of meetings with major political groups to establish a common basis for a national accord. On March 5, the cabinet issued "the 14 Principles for National *Entente*" as a package deal that attempted to meet Christian and Muslim demands and satisfy Damascus. One set of principles, usually voiced by the Christians, affirmed the sovereignty of the state and the formulation of a security plan, the adherence to a free democratic parliamentary system and free economic enterprise, open relations with the international community, the development of relations with the Lebanese abroad, the basing of relations with other countries on mutual respect, and the implementation of agreements made with the PLO. Another set of principles, usually demanded by the Muslims and/or the Lebanese National Movement, asserted the Arab identity of Lebanon, support for the Palestinian cause, rejection of the Camp David Accords, rejection of any cooperation with Israel, and the establishment of a special relationship between Lebanon and Syria.

The next day, the ADF withdrew from East Beirut and its suburbs and was replaced by the Lebanese Army. A Lebanese security plan for further ADF withdrawals did not materialize, however. Moreover, Hoss resigned to allow for the formation of a cabinet of "active forces" to bring about the "national *entente*," but Syria backed off from supporting such a cabinet, and, after many months of consultation, a "second-line" cabinet was formed in October 1980.

The political climate in Lebanon, including the Syrian attitude, changed as a result of three developments. First, Kata'ib militia commander Bashir Gemayel's forceful unification of the Lebanese Forces on July 7, 1980 revived the Palestinian-leftist-Syrian alliance. Walid Junblat, now head of the Lebanese National Movement, called on the Arab world and the Soviet Union to counter this step, and Yasir Arafat declared a general mobilization because he considered the unification "a part of a plan to finish with the Palestinian guerrillas." Damascus considered the unification a prelude to a confessional partition that would lead to the application of the Camp David "conspiracy" after the Palestinian resistance and the Lebanese National Movement were liquidated.

The second development was the conflict that arose between the Shi'a militia, Amal, on the one hand, and the Palestinians and their allies on the other, which turned quickly into violent clashes that started in West Beirut and spread to the south. The confrontation expanded in frequency and intensity amid fears by the Shi'a that the Palestinians were planning to take over the south and establish in it their state. Although the Palestinians denied the charges, the Shi'a read certain of their actions differently: the PLO takeover of all positions in south Lebanon and West Beirut after the ADF withdrawal and its prevention of the Lebanese Army from deployment in these areas, the Palestinian purchase of land in south Lebanon, the PLO funding of the expansion of the port of Sidon, and alleged attempts by the PLO to encourage Shi'a migration from the south to the Beqaa. The same fears were voiced by the Lebanese Front and by government officials, among them, Foreign Minister Fu'ad Butrus in his speech to the UN General Assembly on October 2, 1980:

> We confirm what the president of Lebanon has announced on more than one occasion. We unequivocally reject any plan for implantation [of the Palestinians in the south] and all that may lead to it, directly or indirectly. We shall resist implantation under any cover and in all phases, and we shall resist that with all our power which springs from our belief in our sacred right in our homeland, a right that no one shares with us. By what right and according to what justice do some intend to redress an inequity by a greater injustice, to solve the rightful problem of a people at the expense of another people?

The third development was the polarization in the Arab world because of the Iraq-Iran war, which began in September of 1980, and the emergence of the Syrian-Libyan axis with the announcement of a pact between Syria and Libya, which was countered by an Iraqi-Jordanian axis. Syria intensified its control over Lebanon, to make Lebanon side with it in any regional conflict, and, as a result of such pressure, Lebanon joined Syria in boycotting the Arab summit conference held in Amman on November 25, 1980, which, ironically, opposed Syria's policy of hegemony and pledged to do everything necessary "to create a propitious climate for a Lebanese reconciliation."

Revival of the Arab Follow-up Committee

Despite Lebanon's boycott of the Amman summit, relations between Syria and the Lebanese government and the Lebanese Front continued to worsen. The Lebanese attitude toward the ADF also became more hostile, because of the failure of the ADF to fulfill its mandate. The ADF was supposed to enforce a cease-fire among belligerent parties, support the government in rebuilding its institutions (including the army), and implement the Cairo Accord. Instead, the ADF became, by design or default, a party to the conflict. It was drawn into a series of clashes with the Lebanese Forces in Zahle, which soon degenerated into a full-fledged war marked by intense shelling of the city and severe shortages of food, medical supplies, and public utilities for more than three months. Moreover, Syria opposed the deployment of the Lebanese Army in areas under ADF or PLO control, and the pro-Syrian Lebanese National Movement refused any security role for the Lebanese Army. In addition, fighting broke out between the ADF and the Lebanese Army in Beirut and the Beqaa and was followed by prolonged and intermittant shelling of the army positions in East Beirut and the suburbs. On the southern front, the lenient attitude of the ADF toward the PLO led to their stepping up commando operations, which, in turn, led to an escalation of Israeli reprisals, turning the south into a continuous scene of shelling, air raids, and incursions.

Internally, the Lebanese Front called for total Syrian withdrawal and the Lebanese Forces asked for UN intervention. Externally, some Arab countries (notably, Saudi Arabia and the UAE) called for the inclusion of non-Syrian troops in the ADF. In early April 1981 France launched a limited diplomatic initiative with Syria, Saudi Arabia, Israel, the

United States, and the UN to end the crisis on the basis of a deployment of the Lebanese Army throughout the entire country and the creation of an international peacekeeping force. The proposal was dropped because of Syrian opposition. Similarly, a UN initiative, supported by the United States and France and calling for the appointment of a special representative to help ease the crisis in Lebanon, was blocked by Syria and the Soviet Union.

In the same month, Israel shot down two Syrian helicopters in the Beqaa and flew reconnaissance planes over Syrian positions, prompting Syria to bring in surface-to-air missiles (SAMs). U.S. envoy Philip Habib was then dispatched to the Middle East to deflect the potential conflict with Israel. He and Deputy Assistant Secretary of State Morris Draper shuttled between Lebanon, Syria, and Israel to contain the conflict. Meanwhile they worked out a cease-fire between the PLO and Israel and tried to assist in the process of internal reconciliation.

President Sarkis also tried to resolve the difficulties with the ADF through direct contacts with Syria, but was not able to secure a lasting cease-fire or an approval of a Lebanese security plan that called for the gradual withdrawal of the ADF and the deployment of the Lebanese Army. Once again, fearful of the implications of an internationalization of the conflict, President Sarkis turned to the Arab community for help as he had in October 1980. On June 1, 1981 he called on the Arab Follow-up Committee to resume its efforts to resolve the crisis. The committee convened within a few days and kept meeting on and off until November. During June it concentrated its efforts on a cease-fire and security planning. The committee (particularly the Saudi representative) was instrumental in securing a negotiated settlement for Zahle between the Syrian and the Lebanese Forces, but could not reach an agreement on a security plan because of strong differences of opinion between Syria and the rest of the committee. During the month of July, the committee turned its attention to national *entente*. The Sarkis government presented to the committee a comprehensive plan for the resolution of the Lebanese crisis, including a political program, a schedule for the rehabilitation of the Lebanese Army, a plan for the deployment of the army in the south, and a list of necessary measures to create the appropriate climate for the implementation of the program. The political program detailed the operational measures and the role of Lebanon, Syria, the Arab Follow-up Committee, the PLO, the Lebanese active forces (those that had a military and/or a grass roots political presence), and the UN for the implementation of the following objectives:

1. The final resolution of the issue of collaboration with Israel,

2. A national dialogue for a Lebanese-Lebanese accord,

3. The establishment of wide contacts to allow for the implementation of political and military measures to extend state authority over the south,

4 An agreement on constitutional and political reforms and implementation of the "14-point principles,"

5. The scheduled implementation of agreements with the PLO and the organization of relations with the PLO on that basis,

6. Special relations with Syria.

Syria insisted that the issue of collaboration with Israel be resolved before proceeding with other issues. Consequently, the Lebanese Forces submitted to President Sarkis a paper in which they renounced their ties with Israel. The committee, after discussions with the different parties, met from July 25 to 26 and issued a communiqué in which it expressed satisfaction with the paper presented by the Lebanese Forces and announced the Lebanese government's preparation for a dialogue in which all parties would participate. During the month of September 1981 the committee tried to establish a cease-fire, reopen crossing points in Beirut, and prevent the arrival of new weapons to nongovernment forces by supervising the seaports. The committee attempted for two months to facilitate, through discussions with Syrian officials and

Lebanese parties, the implementation of its resolution. By the November 7 meeting, the situation had not improved. The committee then reaffirmed its earlier resolutions and proposed a security plan based on the deployment of the internal security forces, which were under the direction of the Sunni prime minister, supplemented by army units. The plan was immediately rejected by the Lebanese National Movement, and the committee never met again.

The failure of the Arab Follow-up Committee to reach a solution to the Lebanese crisis, in spite of its determination and prolonged efforts, was the result of inter-Arab disagreements. Arab opposition to Syria's conduct in Lebanon was growing and was demonstrated by the conditional and unenthusiastic approval for the renewal of the mandate of the ADF. Syria had always opposed any Arabization of the Lebanese conflict and was able to turn the only acceptable collective Arab initiative – the ADF – into an instrument of Syrian policy. It was therefore natural for Syria to foil the committee's efforts and discourage the Saudis and Kuwaitis from pursuing their involvement in Lebanon. Both countries withdrew their diplomatic missions from Syrian-controlled West Beirut and pleaded other commitments to avoid further meetings of the committee.

The Fez Summit

The perilous situation in the south and the escalating Palestinian-Israeli conflict there triggered wide diplomatic action both regionally and internationally. As early as July 1981, the Lebanese authorities instructed their representative at the Arab League to ask for an Arab summit that would focus specifically on the issue of the south. When the Fez summit was convened in November of 1981 to discuss the peace plan proposed by Saudi Prince Fahd for the Arab-Israeli conflict, Lebanon submitted a paper on the south. In spite of the disagreement on the Saudi plan, the summit managed to approve unanimously a resolution concerning southern Lebanon that included the following recommendations:

1. Development of a comprehensive Arab plan to end Israeli aggression including the following:
   a. use of political, diplomatic, and economic pressures on all states that can influence Israel,
   b. application of pressure to implement UN resolutions concerning southern Lebanon,
   c. the contribution of each Arab state to the overall strategy according to its ability.

2. Formation of a mini-council of representatives of participants in the summit to draw up a plan for this strategy and submit it to the Arab League Council.

3. Support for the Lebanese government in its deployment of the Lebanese Army in the south and assistance to Lebanon to enable it to resume state functions.

The effect of these resolutions was not any better than those of the Arab Follow-up Committee – and for the same reasons. The Fez summit demonstrated the polarization between the moderate and hard-line Arab states and deepened the conflict between Syria and Saudi Arabia. The Fahd plan marked the beginning of an activist role for Saudi diplomacy and a bid for Saudi leadership in the Arab world after gaining confidence abroad by obtaining the controversial airborne warning and control system (AWACS) airplanes from the United States. Syria, on the other hand, had long considered itself the leading Arab state, and, in opposing the Fahd plan, foiled Saudi Arabia's new regional ambitions. The Saudi setback in Fez made its role as mediator in the Lebanese conflict shaky.

Conclusion

The six years of Arab initiatives, both military and political, contributed very little to the solution of the Lebanese conflict. The basic objectives – security, sovereignty, and unity – were not fulfilled. By 1982 the country was fragmented into eight different zones: (1) the Christian enclave next to the Israeli border controlled by Major Sa'ad Haddad's militia;

(2) the mid-south area controlled by UNIFIL; (3) the rest of the south and the coastal area up to Beirut controlled by the PLO; (4) West Beirut controlled by the PLO, the Lebanese National Movement, and the ADF; (5) the Shouf mountains controlled by the ADF and the Lebanese National Movement; (6) East Beirut, Metn, Kisrwan, and Jubayl controlled by Christian Lebanese Forces; (7) Zghorta and vicinity controlled by the ADF, the forces of Franjieh and the Syrian National Social Party; (8) the north and the Beqaa controlled by the ADF.

The ineffectiveness of the Arab initiative created among the Lebanese a wave of disillusionment with external remedies, a condemnation of foreign intervention, a realization that Lebanon was paying for inter-Arab wars, and a new spirit of Lebanese assertiveness and desire for unity. First, the Shi'a through the Amal movement asserted their independence from the Lebanese National Movement and refused to accept de facto security arrangements taken by the movement or the Syrians in West Beirut or to join in security duties with the PLO. On the contrary, its relations with the PLO in Beirut and the south worsened daily and were marked by serious and continuous clashes in which heavy casualties were incurred. Nabih Barri, secretary general of Amal, summarized the new mood:

> We no longer wish to fight among Lebanese, but for the unity of Lebanon. Our hostility toward the Palestinians is explained in terms of their will to take over state authority. They have not been entrusted to protect our frontiers with Israel. The Lebanese Army alone is entitled to that task. Therefore, we shall call for its deployment in the south and its assumption of PLO positions as well as those of its progressive allies.[10]

Second, the Christian leadership started a series of initiatives to build bridges with the opposition. Bashir Gemayel on November 29, 1981 proposed a plan that aimed at "trans-

ferring the conflict from the military level to the political level
in order to find a realistic solution that would pull Lebanon
out of the crisis." The proposal covered basic principles and
operational measures. The principles included (1) the reestablishment of Lebanese sovereignty over all Lebanese territory,
(2) the withdrawal of Syrian forces and the execution of measures that would preserve the Lebanese territory as a peaceful
neighbor of Syria, (3) the submission of the PLO to Lebanese
authority, and (4) the declaration of a Lebanese consensus
that conflicts would be solved peacefully rather than by force
and that political negotiations would remain the best means
for building a new formula for Lebanese *entente*. The practical measures included

1. Action to preserve the Lebanese identity of the south
by the state's securing all the social, educational, and development services preparatory to the state's restoration of full
sovereignty;
2. The transformation of the Arab Follow-up Committee into an "operational commission" with the task of implementing the following measures by January 15, 1982 in
Beirut:
   a. a final cease-fire;
   b. the withdrawal of the ADF and the PLA;
   c. the formation of a security force composed of and
      commanded by Lebanese active forces; (After nor-
      malizing the situation in Beirut, the committee
      would proceed to deal with the situation in other
      areas of Lebanon, provided it completed its work
      by May 15, 1982.)
3. The formation of a national committee by the president of Lebanon under the chairmanship of the prime minister to carry out negotiations with Syria and the PLO, in
cooperation with the Arab Follow-up Committee, to establish
with them normal and stable relations that would guarantee
the restoration of the full sovereignty and authority of the
Lebanese state.

Although the Lebanese National Movement dismissed the proposal as unworthy of discussion, Amin Gemayel, a Kata'ib party leader, reiterated in January 1982 the readiness of the Kata'ib "to engage in an unconditional dialogue with the leaders of the National Movement." Then, in March, Bashir Gemayel made an appeal to the Muslims for national unity to avoid the dangers of partition or permanent settlement of the Palestinians. "But should the Lebanese Muslims fail to respond favorably, we shall be forced to adopt those decisions required for regaining Lebanon's sovereignty over its land. In doing so, the rights of the Lebanese Muslims — after the victory — will be safeguarded."

Finally, the Sunni leadership began to accuse some Arab states of obstructing the realization of Lebanese *entente*. Former Prime Minister Sa'ib Salam declared in March 1982 that foreign intervention in Lebanon was the cause of the Lebanese conflict, adding that the Lebanese people could settle their problems if they were offered an honest, sincere chance. Furthermore, the political leaders and the 'Ulama (theologians) broke up with the Lebanese National Movement and rejected the latter as representative of the Muslims. When the movement decided in April 1982 to set up local councils in the areas it controlled, the Muslim coalition opposed the move. A noted opponent of the scheme, Shaykh Assaf, president of the Islamic Federation of 'Ulama, was murdered the same month, which triggered a show of internal solidarity. A nationwide strike took place and leaders of all the communities condemned the assassination. The Sunni mufti called the strike the beginning of national accord, and the Maronite patriarch called on Christians and Muslims to unite and take their destiny into their own hands.

10

Phase IV. The Balance of the Occupation: The Israeli Initiative (1982)

Lebanon has never posed a military threat to Israel, and Israel has never claimed any rights to Lebanese territories. Relations between the two countries have been governed by an armistice agreement concluded in 1949. All through the Arab-Israeli conflict, Lebanon has taken the Arab side politically, but it was not involved operationally in the Arab-Israeli wars nor has it acted militarily as a confrontation state although it is a party to the Common Arab Defense Treaty. So Israel's armed conflict was not with Lebanon as an entity but as a territory. The emergence of the PLO in the 1960s and the expansion of its operations in the 1970s turned southern Lebanon into a confrontation zone between the Palestinians and the Israelis. The Israeli Labor Party, with its emphasis on basic national security, apparently did not consider the PLO's presence in Lebanon a threat. Its reaction to PLO activities was limited to retaliatory action and support for Major Haddad's forces in the south so that a buffer zone would be created between the PLO and Israel. When the Syrian troops moved into Lebanon in 1976, Israel did not object, although it had previously opposed the deployment of any Arab army into another country neighboring Israel. The Labor government considered such a deployment advantageous in that it would disperse the Syrian Army and, perhaps equally important, control the Palestinian resistance so that the political-strategic status quo in Lebanon would be preserved. The *Washington Post* on May 14, 1981 maintained that, through U.S. mediation, a tacit agreement was made between Israel and Syria, wherein, Syria, in return for the deployment of its forces in Lebanon without Israeli interference, agreed not to interfere "in Israeli ground operations or air strikes against Palestinian guerrilla positions, particularly those south of the Zahrani river." Other conditions included "no movement of Syrian troops south of the Zahrani; no deployment of Syrian missiles in Lebanon; no Syrian attempt to close the Christian port of Junieh; and no imbalance in the Syrian moves against the Christians and Palestinians."

The Likud government that came to power in 1977 seemed to be concerned not only with basic national security but also with the country's current security, which was endangered by the PLO harrassment of northern Israel. It was no longer satisfied with retaliation for PLO attacks but wanted to keep the PLO off balance, decrease its military and political potential, and ultimately disable it. Within this policy framework Prime Minister Menachem Begin's government launched the "Litani operation" in March 1978, the preemptive strike strategy in 1979, the massive air strikes in August 1980, the air strikes in southern Lebanon, the naval shelling of Palestinian camps near Tripoli in June 1981, and the massive air bombardment of the PLO infrastructure in July 1981. The Likud government also viewed the Syrian presence in Lebanon in more negative terms than the Labor government had, perceiving it in the context of a zero-sum game.

Defense Minister Ariel Sharon brought with his appointment in the summer of 1981 a deeper ideological and strategic dimension to the problem. He reasoned that the long-term strategic requirements of Israel's national security and that of its northern border demanded a change in approach toward the three major elements on the Lebanese scene: The PLO, Syria, and the Lebanese government. First, the PLO had to be completely uprooted from Lebanon – particularly from Beirut – which would discredit its leadership and weaken its political grip over the West Bank. Moderate Palestinians would then emerge and seek accommodation with Israel. Second, Israel had made a mistake in allowing the Syrians into Lebanon. The Syrian troops should be evicted from Lebanon to prevent any interference in the political process. Finally, fundamental changes in Lebanon's political status had to take place in the form of a strong central regime friendly to Israel and capable of preventing future terrorism. The three objectives were apparently interrelated by Sharon, who was quoted as saying: "A government of that kind cannot come into being as long as the terrorists control southern Lebanon and two-thirds of the city of Beirut and as long as the Syrians control whole sections of Lebanon."[11]

As early as December 1981, when Israel annexed the Golan Heights, Sharon reportedly tried to get the approval of the Israeli cabinet for a war plan, "Operation Big Pines," that entailed the invasion of Lebanon all the way to the Beirut-Damascus highway if the Syrians reacted militarily to the annexation. Although there was no support for such a large-scale action, the military planning proceeded, and by March 1982 the operational plans were well advanced. According to one Israeli version, D-Day was scheduled for Sunday May 17 but was postponed because there was not enough political support for such a major ground action for the following reasons:

1. A clash with the Syrians was inevitable. Syria would throw in the full weight of its air force which would make it imperative for Israel to attack the Syrian missiles, thereby escalating the confrontation even further.

2. The Christians would not intervene to assist the Israelis. They might even denounce the Israeli attack to preserve their Arab credentials.

3. This operation could not destroy the terrorists because they would reorganize elsewhere.

4. Israel was divided on this issue.

5. When, in the aftermath of the operation, the subject of the sovereignty of Lebanon was discussed, Israel would

have to give up its support for the Lebanese Forces in the north and Major Haddad in the south, and the subject of the Golan Heights and West Bank would be raised.[12]

In spite of this attitude, when the Israeli ambassador was attacked in London on June 3, 1982, Israel retaliated the next day by bombing PLO targets in West Beirut, knowing that the PLO would respond by firing on the settlements in northern Israel. When this happened, Israel launched a large-scale incursion into Lebanon – "Peace for Galilee" – with an announced target of 40 kilometers to ensure that northern Israel would be beyond the range of PLO artillery fire. By June 11, however, the Israeli Defense Force (IDF) had controlled all the area south of Beirut except the Beirut-Damour-Aley triangle, and by June 13 the IDF linked up with the area under the control of the Lebanese Forces in Ba'abda, thus encircling West Beirut. In another drive from June 21 to 25, the IDF took control of the Aley area up to Bhamdoun.

Did the Israeli invasion fulfill Sharon's objectives for the three players on the Lebanese scene, namely the PLO, the Syrian forces, and the Lebanese "friends"?

Israel vs. Syria

In the first few days of the invasion, Israel repeatedly affirmed that it had no desire to attack Syrian forces in Lebanon. The Syrians also took precautionary measures to demonstrate that they wanted no part in the war, particularly because these forces were deployed in a police rather than a combat configuration. On June 7, 1982, Begin asked U.S. envoy Philip Habib to assure President Assad that Israel was not planning to attack Syrian forces but that it demanded the removal of the SAMs from the Beqaa and the withdrawal of PLO fighters and equipment located in the Beqaa within 40 kilometers of the Israeli border. By the time Habib met Assad on June 10, the missiles had been destroyed by Israeli raids and Syrian ground forces had been attacked.

Sharon's objective was to cut the Beirut-Damascus highway to prevent Syria from controlling Beirut and imposing
a puppet regime on the Lebanese. He first tried to reach the
Beirut-Damacus highway through the upper Shouf at Mudayrij junction before the Syrians could rally enough force
to stop the offensive. Time was, therefore, of the essence. But
the column that was supposed to reach Mudayrij was delayed
by military and logistic setbacks, and by the time it reached
Ayn Zhalta the Syrians were well prepared and ready in Ayn
Dara, and one of the deadliest battles of the war took place,
bringing the Israeli advance to a standstill fewer than 10
kilometers from its destination.

After the Ayn Zhalta halt, Sharon's next possibility was
to cut the Beirut-Damascus highway in the Beqaa near Shtou-
ra. Once again the IDF column was unable to arrive before
a cease-fire was announced on Friday, June 11. On June 13
the highway was cut right above Beirut in the vicinity of
Ba'abda, and later on, using the technique of a "creeping
cease-fire," the IDF reached Bhamdoun, and, through a final assault on June 25, secured the Beirut-Damascus road
from Beirut to the outskirts of Sofar. But Beirut remained
within Syrian artillery range and its government subject to
Syrian "intervention."

Israel vs. the PLO

Israel succeeded in a few days in seizing all the major Palestinian strongholds south of Beirut and controlling the area
once occupied by the Palestinians. The PLO fighters could
not stop the Israeli advance and consequently withdrew to
West Beirut. Israel was determined to uproot the PLO from
Beirut as well and had two options: to force its way in or accept negotiations through U.S. envoy Habib. It opted for the
latter, but not without applying pressure — a seige of the city
and heavy artillery shelling and air strikes. The PLO leadership held out at first and even talked of turning Beirut into
another Stalingrad. But when the IDF tightened the seige

and persisted in its massive shelling – while the Arab countries refrained from any aid – Arafat entered into the negotiation process with Habib through Lebanon's Prime Minister Shafiq Wazzan. The nine-point plan that Habib used as a framework for his negotiations consisted of the following items:

1. Cease-fire in place.
2. All PLO leaders are to leave Lebanon under assurances of safe passage.
3. All PLO fighters in Beirut are to leave Lebanon without their heavy weapons, but individual sidearms will be permitted. Departure, again, will be under assurances of safe passage.
4. There will be no redeployment of any armed PLO fighters from Beirut to other locations in Lebanon.
5. A PLO political presence in Lebanon is acceptable, but preferably not in Beirut.
6. A readjustment of Israeli Defense Force (IDF) lines will take place after an agreement is reached and as implementation is well underway.
7. The Lebanese Armed Forces will take control of all of Beirut.
8. Other armed elements in West Beirut would turn over their arms to the Lebanese Armed Forces. The Syrian Arab Deterrent Forces (ADF) and associated units will return to Syria.
9. Related to the above, but not linked to the West Beirut issue, it is a matter of policy that in the final arrangements there will be no foreign military presence in Lebanon, be it PLO, Syrian, or Israeli.

As Habib continued his negotiations with the immediate parties and with Arab and European governments to find host countries for the PLO fighters and leaders and to assemble a multinational force (MNF), which would supervise their evacuation and safe passage, Israel continued its military pressure by escalating its bombardment and advancing

into the southern suburbs of Beirut. By mid-August Habib
was able to secure agreement on the elements of a "Plan for
the Departure from Lebanon of the PLO Leadership, Offices,
and Combatants in Beirut." The plan's basic concept was that

> all the PLO, leadership, offices, and combatants in Bei-
> rut will leave Lebanon peacefully for prearranged desti-
> nations in other countries, in accord with the departure
> schedules and arrangements set out in this plan. The
> basic concept in this plan is consistent with the objec-
> tive of the government of Lebanon that all foreign mili-
> tary forces withdraw from Lebanon.

The plan was approved by the PLO and the Lebanese cabinet
on August 18 and by the Israeli cabinet the next day. The
plan envisaged that the evacuation would be completed by
September 3, 1982, after which the MNF would assist the
Lebanese Armed Forces "in arrangements, as may be agreed
between governments concerned, to ensure good and lasting
security throughout the area of operation," until its departure between September 21–26. As planned, advance elements
of the MNF arrived on August 21 and the first contingent
of PLO fighters left by ship. In the next 10 days more than
6,000 PLO fighters were evacuated from Beirut by sea and
over land. Arafat himself left on August 30 for Tunis via
Greece. The PLO state-within-a-state was finally dismantled,
and the Lebanese Army was deployed into certain parts of
West Beirut for the first time since 1975. The U.S. marines of
the MNF left Beirut September 10, the Italians September 11,
and the French September 14, well ahead of their schedule.

Israel vs. Lebanese "Friends"

Sharon expected a warm welcome and an open endorsement
by the Lebanese Christians, especially after the Israeli invasion had "liberated" them from any Palestinian or Syrian
threat. He even wanted the Lebanese Forces to link with his
troops and fight the PLO in West Beirut. Some Israelis, how-

ever, suspected that although the Christians wanted Israel to come and "liberate" the country, they would not associate with them either because of their Arab affiliation or, as pragmatists, fear of Arab reprisals. Some Israelis were even reluctant to enter into the war because they believed that the Christians would use them as tools to purge Lebanon of the Palestinians and Syrians and then would maintain their allegiance to the Arab world.[13] In fact, the Lebanese Forces refused to be directly involved or even associated with the Israelis. They publicly attributed the Israeli invasion to Israel's national security interests and not in any way to a "deal" with the Lebanese. Moreover, Bashir Gemayel continued to build bridges to the other Lebanese communities, something he had started a few months earlier. Once he decided he wanted to be president of a united Lebanon—not a Christian mini-state—through the constitutional process, he could not afford to be tainted in the view of the Lebanese Muslims or the other Arabs. His public response to the Israeli invasion was a call for the liberation of Lebanon from all occupying forces: "As far as we are concerned, we are looking for the liberation of our country. We are looking for *all* the foreigners to leave—Syrians, Palestinians, Israelis, and even UNIFIL—we don't need any foreign armed presence in this country." Camille Chamoun, the head of the Lebanese Front, voiced the same sentiment: "In the face of this tragedy, we pledge to do everything we can to turn these events in favor of Lebanon and its people and to secure Lebanon's total sovereignty and the liberation of its territory from all foreigners without exception."

The independent position of the Christian leadership before and after Bashir Gemayel's election, led some Israeli officers, according to authors Ze'ev Schiff and Ehud Ya'ari, to consider a complete turnabout in Israeli policy that involved (1) concentrating on the creation of a security zone in the south by strengthening Major Haddad's forces and developing good relations with the Shi'a and (2) reaching a tacit agreement with Syria on partitioning the country into zones of influence, with Israel controlling the south, Syria taking over the Beqaa and north, and Bashir Gemayel presiding over a central Christian enclave.[14]

A New Hope

For the first time in six years, the Lebanese felt that there was a real opportunity to save Lebanon and restore its sovereignty. In spite of the heavy casualties, devastation, and the entry of an additional foreign occupying force, there was a new hope that maybe the conflict had become big enough to demand a drastic solution and that the balanced occupation would trigger a total withdrawal. This hope created new political dynamics, and the different communal views started to converge quickly on three basic principles: (1) the restoration of Lebanon's sovereignty and territorial integrity through the withdrawal of all foreign forces – Palestinians, Syrians, and Israelis, the disarmament of the Palestinian camps, and the enforcement of the law equally for all residents; (2) the revitalization of the political process toward the achievement of national unity; and (3) the establishment of a strong central government.

The call for the withdrawal of all foreign forces brought up the issue of the mandate and legitimacy of the ADF. For the first time the Lebanese cabinet took a united position regarding foreign forces and voiced on July 14 its support for the government efforts to assure the withdrawal of all non-Lebanese armed forces. When the mandate of the ADF expired on July 28, President Sarkis refused to request its renewal, and later, on September 6, requested at the Arab summit in Fez the withdrawal of ADF. The summit, however, endorsed the Syrian position in its final resolution: "The summit was informed of the Lebanese government's decision to end the mission of ADF in Lebanon. To this effect, the Lebanese and Syrian Governments will start negotiation on measures to be taken in light of the Israeli withdrawal from Lebanon." Lebanon expressed reservations about this resolution, as it wanted its own paper adopted, which called for Syrian withdrawal as an independent act.

The revitalization of the political process was a difficult task because it was now the turn of the Lebanese factions who were allied with the Palestinians and who counted on their support in the internal power struggle to feel threatened by the injection of an external element – the Israeli presence – into the internal political system. In an attempt to turn this destabilizing factor into a force for unification, President Sarkis formed a Council of National Salvation on June 14 that included Prime Minister Shafiq Wazzan, Foreign Minister Fu'ad Butrus, Deputy Nasri Ma'louf, and the leaders of active forces – Bashir Gemayel, Nabih Barri, and Walid Junblat. (Junblat participated only upon the insistence of U.S. envoy Habib.) The council met only twice (on June 20 and 22) to deliberate the withdrawal of foreign forces and deployment of the Lebanese army. On June 24, Junblat announced his resignation from the council and political life.

The drive for the establishment of a strong central regime was demonstrated by the election of Bashir Gemayel as president of Lebanon on August 23, 1982 by a majority vote of a duly constituted quorum in Parliament. Eighty-four percent of the Christian deputies and 46 percent of the Muslim deputies voted, and Gemayel received 57 of the 62 votes cast. Bashir was perceived as a strong, energetic, and decisive leader who could restore to the country its unity, legality, sovereignty, and dignity.

The momentum for a new beginning was strengthened by U.S. policy and involvement. At the outset of the Israeli invasion, U.S. Secretary of State Alexander Haig anticipated changes in the political equilibrium in Lebanon and a substantial reduction of the Syrian presence. Later on, President Ronald Reagan articulated the U.S. objectives in Lebanon as "a permanent cessation of hostilities; establishment of a strong, representative, central government; withdrawal of all foreign forces; restoration of control by the Lebanese government throughout the country, and establishment of conditions under which Lebanon no longer can be used as a launching point for attacks against Israel." Habib and his colleagues were deeply involved in the fulfillment of these objectives, and their contribution was decisive in securing cease-fires, the PLO evacuation from Beirut, and the revival of the political process including the formation of the Council of National Salvation and the election of a president within constitutional procedures. The U.S. involvement, perceived as an act of faith in Lebanon and its future, reinforced the hopes of the Lebanese.

Hopes were, however, shattered when on September 14 President-elect Gemayel was assassinated along with 26 others by a bomb that exploded above his party office in East Beirut. His death triggered four events. First, in the words of his brother Amin,

> after eight years of crisis, difficulties, murder, and destruction, all the Lebanese communities are here today in Bikfaya, around the coffin of Bashir Gemayel. Representatives from all the regions of Lebanon – Sunnis, Maronites, Shi'a, Greek Orthodox, Druze, and Greek Catholic – are here in Bikfaya to affirm that the blood of Bashir Gemayel did not run in vain, but was shed for the unity of Lebanon and dignity of its people.

Second, the Israeli forces went into West Beirut claiming they were there "to prevent any rise in tension and preserve calm following the assassination." Third, the Lebanese cabinet called for the return of the MNF. Fourth, the United States initiated a strategy based on a limited but highly symbolic use of force, and, with Bashir's death, the United States lost the initiative and began to react to events.

Lebanon emerged from this phase more united. Even the Sabra and Shatila camp massacres could not reverse the unification trend, and the Muslim leadership refused to lay the blame on the Christian Lebanese Forces. But in the domain of sovereignty there was no progress. The territories that were occupied by the PLO and the ADF were now occupied by the PLO, the ADF, and the IDF.

11

Phase V. Withdrawals First: The U.S. Partnership (1982–1983)

The momentum for unity and peace, which was disrupted by Bashir Gemayel's tragic death, was revived by the election, one week later, of his brother Amin by an overwhelming majority of the Parliament (77 votes and 3 abstentions). Amin Gemayel, who took office on September 23, enjoyed good relations with both Christian and Muslim leaders in Lebanon and the majority of Arab countries as well. The Christians identified with him as a leader of the Lebanese resistence against Palestinian aggression in 1975–1976 and as an adherer to his brother's vision. The Muslims considered him a moderate leader who maintained open channels of dialogue with the opposition, the PLO, and Syria and one who did not subscribe to violence as a political tool. The majority welcomed him as a seasoned development-oriented politician who had built his reputation on, among other things, modernizing his Metn district and founding the "House of the Future," a documentation and research center for political and social development.

Unlike any other president, Amin Gemayel inherited two presidencies. From President Sarkis, he received the full responsibility for a country controlled by a multitude of foreign and local forces, divided politically and psychologically, and threatened with disintegration and partition. From President-

Elect Bashir Gemayel he inherited the full burden of all the hopes and dreams for a liberated, strong, and proud country triggered by Bashir's election – and the shattered hopes and the dreams-turned-nightmares by his death. Unlike any other president, he had no internal opposition and enjoyed the support of all the Arab world and the Western nations. The MNF returned to Beirut between September 24 and 29 under President Reagan's reported instructions that the U.S. marines would stay in Lebanon until all foreign forces left and the Lebanese government requested their departure. All these factors allowed President Gemayel in the first week of his presidency to unify Beirut after securing the withdrawal of the IDF from West Beirut and the deployment of the MNF and the Lebanese Army in the city.

President Gemayel's agenda for Lebanon centered on four objectives: (1) security: stopping the cycle of violence, destruction, and bloodshed; (2) unity: "the homeland's primary need is the unity of its sons," for "without national unity there is no nation"; (3) sovereignty: the withdrawal of all foreign forces and loyalty to Lebanon – "Dual loyalty can never be accepted and neither can we accept partners in our land"; and (4) reconstruction of the country: physical reconstruction, the revival of governmental institutions, and the modernization of public administration. To achieve these objectives, he considered national consensus necessary but not sufficient, because the multidimensional nature of the conflict necessitated a combination of domestic and foreign initiatives. His first major action was to take the Lebanese cause to where it mattered: the UN, Europe, and the United States.

President Gemayel's first trip to the United States in October 1982 signaled a new era of active partnership in the U.S.-Lebanese relations, based on a convergence of policies in support of the "unity, territorial integrity, and liberty of Lebanon." President Gemayel emphasized (1) the immediate and unconditional withdrawal of all non-Lebanese forces from Lebanon; (2) Lebanon's responsibility for providing security over its land by building an army along "national, equitable, and rational lines"; (3) Lebanon's intent to live in peace and freedom internally and with its neighbors; and (4) Lebanon's peacemaking role in the Middle East after regaining its freedom and stability. President Reagan reconfirmed U.S. support for Lebanon, stating that "President Gemayel deserves our full support at a time when he and his people are working for the reconstruction of Lebanon."

Withdrawal and Negotiations: Policy Options

The Lebanese leadership assumed that the internal conflict was over and that a national political consensus now existed. A government of technocrats was formed on October 7 to bring normalcy to the country and its institutions and oversee reconstruction and development. The government requested, and was granted by Parliament, exceptional legislative powers in the areas of defense, security, public safety, social affairs, health, economy, finance, education, information, reconstruction, and development. The restoration of national sovereignty by the ending of any non-Lebanese military presence was given highest priority, based on the conviction that without this no other national objective could be fully realized or maintained. Consequently, the U.S.-Lebanese partnership concentrated on achieving withdrawals of foreign forces as a continuation of the earlier efforts of U.S. envoy Habib, which had culminated in the PLO evacuation from Beirut. Lebanon considered the PLO withdrawal a first step in a series of U.S.-mediated negotiations that involved Lebanon, the PLO, Syria, and Israel and resulted in Habib's nine-point agreement in which the ninth point — "there will be no foreign military presence in Lebanon, be it PLO, Syrian, or Israeli" — was the unfinished business.

The situation proved to be much more complex than anticipated, however, particularly because Israel insisted on direct negotiations. Lebanon (and the United States) ended with an unprecedented situation: negotiating for the withdrawal of forces of three parties that demanded they be approached and treated differently for ideological and historical reasons. Yet their withdrawals were interrelated in that the process and product of negotiations with any party would effect the possibility and outcome of negotiations with the others. But they refused to sit at the same table or negotiate simultaneously. Under these impossible conditions, and assuming a sincere desire for withdrawals, Lebanon and the United States had to find "the precise formula" that would satisfy Syria, the PLO, and Israel simultaneously. For these reasons, Lebanon had to "linearize" the negotiations and start with the Israeli dimension because, in Arab thinking, Israel was the aggressor and the Fez summit implied a sequence when it proposed that arrangements for Syrian withdrawal were to be made in light of an Israeli withdrawal. Moreover, Damascus insisted in its contacts with Beirut and Washington that it refused to be equated with Israel and that Syria would never be an obstacle to the withdrawals. Once the issue of Israeli occupation was resolved, Syria would respond positively to any official Lebanese request to withdraw. The issue, President Assad stated in November 1982, was that "from 1976 until now, no Lebanese official has asked us, by hint or by statement, to withdraw from Lebanon, or told us, 'we do not want you in Lebanon.'"

Lebanon believed negotiations with Israel were the only available way to secure its liberation. Other options were not viable: no national or Arab military force was available, UN resolutions proved ineffective in the long Israeli occupation of Arab territories, and "just waiting" while the whole country was under foreign control risked the very essence of the nation and the vital fabric of society. The limits for negotiations were clearly defined from the outset and later articulated by President Gemayel before the Non-Aligned summit in New Delhi in March 1983:

1. Lebanon must preserve its national consensus. Lebanon is committed to take positions that emerge from the will of the people;
2. Lebanon cannot violate the principle of national

sovereignty; it cannot grant privileges to anyone, and it cannot accept the presence of any foreign military force on its territory;

3. Lebanon cannot endanger its credibility in the Arab world, its association with the Arab community of states, and its creative role in the region.

Clearly Lebanon negotiated with Israel within the framework of Arab political requirements (and specifically Syrian ones). Interim negotiation results were always tested against a perceived Syrian or Arab position. If this self-imposed constraint had not existed, the negotiations could have been concluded in 10 days.

The Dynamics of Negotiation

Negotiations for Israeli troop withdrawals were started on December 28, 1982 in Khalde (near Beirut) after many weeks of hard bargaining over the place, level, and scope of negotiations. The Lebanese team was headed by Antoine Fattal, a retired career diplomat, the Israeli team by David Kimche, director general of the Ministry of Foreign Affairs, and the U.S. team by Morris Draper, deputy assistant secretary of state. It took another two weeks and five sessions of negotiations to agree on an agenda comprising the termination of the state of war, security arrangements, the framework for mutual relations, a program for total withdrawals, and possible guarantees.

Each party entered the negotiations from a different perspective. Lebanon maintained that it did not enter into a war with Israel, and, therefore, should not be asked to pay for another party's defeat, namely the PLO's. Consequently, the 1949 armistice agreement continued to be valid and, if necessary, could be modified or replaced by a similar security agreement to guarantee that the Lebanese territory would not be used for acts of aggression against Israel. Lebanon sought peace but could not achieve it alone because it was bound by interregional relations. Finally, Lebanon requested full and fast withdrawals of all foreign forces within a comprehensive and programmed plan.

Although Israel affirmed that the purpose of negotiations was not to end a conflict with Lebanon, because there had never been one, it considered the 1949 armistice agreement null when Lebanon concluded the Cairo Accord, which permitted the PLO to wage war against Israel from Lebanon. Israel assumed that the "eradication" of the PLO presence from Beirut would open the way for special relations with Lebanon based on friendship and security. The "opening bid" was a cabinet resolution of October 10, 1982 consisting of the following points:

1. Israel seeks a peace treaty with Lebanon.
2. The government of Israel proposes the immediate start of negotiations for the withdrawal of all foreign forces from Lebanon.
3. The first to leave will be the PLO terrorists still remaining in the Beqaa valley and in northern Lebanon.
4. The Syrian army and the IDF will leave Lebanon simultaneously.
5. All Israeli POW's, soldiers missing in action and the bodies of fallen soldiers will be delivered to the IDF before the IDF leaves Lebanon.
6. Security arrangements will be made prior to departure to ensure that Lebanon will not serve again as a base for hostile actions against Israel.

The United States participated technically as a witness but actually as a mediator, upon the insistence of Lebanon. The United States supported Lebanon's independence, territorial integrity, and full sovereignty over all its territory as well as Israel's legitimate demand for security. During negotiations U.S.-Israeli relations were not at their best for at least two reasons. First, Israel would have preferred bilateral negotiations because the U.S. presence provided Lebanon with an umbrella, an option, and an arbitrator. The confron-

tation of Habib with an alleged Lebanese-Israeli agreement—
the "Sharon paper" of December 14, 1982—was an attempt
to bypass the U.S. channel and underlined the need to accel-
erate the formalization of the tripartite negotiations. Sharon's
personality was also a very large factor in U.S.-Israeli negotiations. Second, Reagan's Middle East peace initiative of
September 1, 1982 linked the withdrawal of forces from Lebanon to an overall resolution of the root causes of the Arab-
Israeli conflict. Israel rejected the Reagan initiative because
it was contrary to Israel's design to make the West Bank an
integral part of Israel. A quick U.S. success in Lebanon would
short-circuit Israeli plans and improve the U.S. potential for
imposing a regional settlement. The United States had similar problems with Syria, whose initial reaction to Reagan's
plan was sharply negative because the Golan Heights were
not explicitly included, and because the plan was basically
the Camp David Accords, with Jordan speaking for the Palestinians. Even when assured that the plan related to the
Golan, Damascus still believed that the Golan would not be
returned to Syria, and, in the process of implementing the
initiative, Syria's regional leverage would erode because more
elements of the Arab-Israeli conflict would have been resolved.
Moreover, Syria was anxious, along with the Soviets, to deprive the United States of a diplomatic success.

Negotiations were going very slowly, and the Lebanese
government suspected that they were being held hostage to
block Reagan's peace initiative. I was dispatched to Washington in February 1983 to discuss with the U.S. administration the desirability of decoupling the Lebanese problem from
the regional one. I argued that

> regaining Lebanon's freedom is important in itself, just
> as the solution of the Palestinian problem is important
> in itself also. In fact, arbitrary linkage either forces so-
> lution of the complex Palestinian issue into the urgent,
> collapsing time frame of Lebanon's deterioration under
> occupation or forces Lebanon's continued occupation
> and de facto partition by chaining Lebanon's freedom to

the eventual solution of the Palestinian problem. While the two issues are interrelated, the treatment of each of them should have a life of its own in terms of time, conditions, and tradeoffs.

Meanwhile, President Reagan suggested that Israel was delaying withdrawals unnecessarily. "For them not to leave now," he asserted, "puts them technically in the position of an occupying force."

By March 1983 talks were stalling because of Israel's insistence on leaving behind a military presence in the form of observation posts and joint patrols and on securing a visible degree of normalization with Lebanon. An Israeli delegation led by Yitzhak Shamir visited Washington on March 10 to gain support for the Israeli position. A day later, a delegation of high ranking Lebanese officials (including former Prime Minister Sa'ib Salam) arrived in Washington for consultations to break the impasse in negotiations. The United States was sympathetic to Israel's security concerns but supportive of Lebanon's rejection of any infringement on its sovereignty. In an effort to reconcile the two positions, new ideas were explored, such as a tripartite military commission, joint Lebanese-Israeli supervisory teams to verify security arrangements, the absorption of Major Haddad's troops into the army, a U.S. presence in southern Lebanon directly or through the MNF, accelerated U.S. training of antiterrorism units of the Lebanese Army, increased military aid to Israel and Lebanon, and the expansion of UNIFIL's role.

In April, the negotiation process made some progress. Negotiating subcommittees were formed to intensify discussion on the various agenda items. On April 12 Habib joined the negotiations, and, despite the bombing of the U.S. embassy on April 18, negotiations continued, and on April 23 President Reagan announced that he was sending Secretary of State George Shultz to the Middle East to assist in the peace process. Shultz had to resolve three major issues: the future status of Major Haddad, the mode of supervision of security in southern Lebanon, and the degree of normalization between Lebanon and Israel. Shultz shuttled between Lebanon and Israel and was able to complete a draft agreement that was accepted by Lebanon on May 4 and by the Israeli cabinet "in principle" on May 6 – with a request for about 15 clarifications, which were rejected by Lebanon because they were no more than redrafts of earlier Israeli demands.

Shultz then visited Syria, Jordan, and Saudi Arabia to enlist Arab support for the agreement. Both Jordan and Saudi Arabia confirmed Lebanon's right to conclude any agreement that it believed served its national interest, while Syria introduced a different dimension: "We consider any gain realized by the Israeli invasion a threat to our national and Arab security, which will force us to stay in Lebanon as long as these gains remain." When Foreign Minister Elie Salem carried the text of the agreement to Damascus on May 12, it was rejected in substance and form as a "submissive contract." President Gemayel expressed deep concern about Syria's position, which could have resulted in an agreement and no withdrawals, and Secretary Shultz emphasized that Syria should not be allowed to exercise a veto power, especially because President Assad had not slammed the door shut during their discussions. The Lebanese cabinet went ahead and unanimously approved the agreement on May 14 and authorized Fattal to sign. The agreement was approved by the Israeli Knesset on May 16 and signed on May 17. The Lebanese Parliament, after lengthy debates, decided by a vast majority (65 to 2) on June 14, to license the government to ratify the agreement.

The agreement gave Lebanon a guarantee against any Israeli territorial claims, considering "the existing international boundaries between Lebanon and Israel inviolable," a commitment for a full Israeli withdrawal within 8 to 12 weeks, full control over the south with no residual Israeli military presence, a disengagement from the Arab-Israeli conflict, termination of the state of war with each party to refrain "from using the territory of the other party for conducting a military attack against the territory of a third state," and the ability to check security arrangements on the Israeli side of the border.

On the other hand, the agreement met Israel's overriding demand for the security of its northern border. In addition to a general commitment that Lebanon's territory would not be used as a base for hostile or terrorist activity against the territory or people of Israel, some specific security arrangements were stipulated. A security region was delineated in which the Lebanese authorities would enforce special security measures aimed at detecting and preventing potential hostile activities against Israel and within which certain arms limitations would be imposed. The implementation of these arrangements was entrusted to a Joint Security Arrangements Committee, which would have the authority to establish and operate Joint Supervisory Teams to verify the implementation of these arrangements, "in recognition of the fact that the responsibility for military, police, and other control operations rests with the Lebanese Armed Forces, police, and other authorized Lebanese organizations, and not with the teams." The agreement, however, fell short of Israel's demands for a peace treaty and normalization of relations. Lebanon only agreed to a Joint (tripartite) Liaison Committee that would address itself to the development of mutual relations and "would initiate, within six months of the total Israeli withdrawal, *bona fide* negotiations in order to conclude agreements on the movement of goods, products, and persons and their implementation on a non-discriminatory basis."

Israel, in a side letter to the United States, linked its withdrawal to the return of Israeli prisoners held by Syria and the PLO and the bodies of soldiers killed since June 4, 1982, and to the simultaneous withdrawal of Syrian troops and remaining PLO fighters. If these conditions were not met, Israel reserved the right to suspend implementation of the agreement or consider it null. This prompted Lebanon to confirm its position in a similar letter that unless the Israeli withdrawals took place in accordance with the terms of the agreement, Lebanon would be at liberty to suspend per-formance of its obligations under the agreement and ultimately declare the agreement null and void. Both letters, however, affirmed that prior to any such action "Lebanon, the United States and Israel will consult on an urgent basis." The United States merely acknowledged these positions and, in a May 17, 1983 letter from President Reagan to President Gemayel, expressed its commitment to the implementation of the agreement by using its best efforts to bring about the withdrawal of all external forces and to avoid action that might be taken by any regional power to prevent the implementation of the agreement or otherwise harm Lebanon.

Impasse and Dilemma

Lebanon consciously tried to keep the Arab world informed of the progress of negotiations. When the agreement was concluded, cabinet ministers toured the Arab countries to explain the agreement and solicit support for it. Egypt, Jordan, Sudan, Algeria, Iraq, and Morocco proclaimed their initial support. Saudi Arabia and the Gulf Cooperation Council expressed their respect for Lebanon's right to make such decisions. Some Arab leaders privately conveyed their approval but were not willing to make public statements of support. The two parties that were linked to the Israeli withdrawal, however, rejected the agreement. The PLO opposed it and warned the Lebanese government "against delineating any borders with the Zionist enemy, since the legitimate right to delineate borders with Lebanon belongs to the Palestinian people," and Syria took an uncompromising position against the substance of the agreement as well as against withdrawing within its framework.

Syria's opposition, which escalated sharply from a criticism of the agreement to an attack on the Lebanese government, was based on four considerations. First, Syria maintained that the agreement violated Lebanon's sovereignty, particularly where it stipulated the formation of Joint Supervisory Teams, and created a disequilibrium in the internal

Lebanese formula in favor of the Christians. Damascus claimed that when disequilibrium occurred in 1976 in favor of pro-Palestinian groups, it intervened militarily to restore the equilibrium. In deciding what was acceptable for Lebanon, Syria was trying to regain the initiative, which it had enjoyed until the Israeli invasion, and play the decisive role in the Lebanese political process. Second, Syria considered the agreement a threat to its national security. Third, ideologically Syria projected itself as a champion of the Palestinian and Arab cause and any step-by-step settlement with Israel would leave the Palestinians with little leverage. Damascus considered the agreement similar to the Camp David Accords by taking an Arab country out of the Arab-Israeli conflict in violation of Arab solidarity and commitments. "Terminating the state of war," Syrian Foreign Minister Khaddam asserted, "is an Arab responsibility, and we believe that neither Lebanon nor the Lebanese government has the right to yield to Israeli pressure and terminate the state of war." Finally, Syria, for international and regional considerations, had every reason to deny the U.S. a diplomatic victory, from its rejection of the Reagan peace initiative to its perception of being left out from the Lebanese negotiations.

Syria's opposition to the agreement created a four-dimensional impasse. First, Syria refused to withdraw from Lebanon on the basis of the agreement, which made Israel refuse to withdraw, in turn, because it linked its withdrawal to the Syrian withdrawal – which gave Syria another reason for not withdrawing. (It was assumed that the PLO would withdraw because of its dependence on the Syrian presence.) Hence, Lebanon ended with an agreement and a Catch-22 situation. As early as June 6, President Gemayel, in a letter to President Reagan, raised questions about "the wisdom of pursuing the ratification of an agreement that may be unimplementable" – and he never ratified it. Second, Syria's position called into question Lebanon's Arab credibility, commitment, and identity, which placed other Arab countries that wished to support Lebanon in a difficult position. Third, Syria encouraged and supported Lebanese opposition to the agreement, which culminated in the formation of a National Salvation Front on July 23, headed by Suleiman Franjieh, Rashid Karami, and Walid Junblat, the aims of which, according to its charter, were the organization of national opposition to the agreement, the confrontation of the dominance of the Kata'ib party over government institutions, and the consolidation of the territories under Syrian control. Finally, the security situation deteriorated as the shelling of Beirut, Metn, and Kisrwan from Syrian-controlled areas became a daily ritual.

As the Lebanese government was mustering support for the agreement and consulting with the United States to find ways to resolve the impasse, Israel unilaterally decided to pull out from the Aley and Shouf districts. This created a dilemma for Lebanon. On the one hand, any withdrawal of foreign forces was welcomed. On the other hand, an Israeli partial withdrawal created a multitude of problems. First, Israel would have to consolidate its position in the south and exercise a heavy hand to minimize its casualties – which would make the region look like a "North Bank," an area that appeared to be partitioned or annexed. Second, the withdrawal, not being part of a schedule of full withdrawal, raised questions about the credibility and usefulness of the agreement and made the Lebanese government look as if it were a party to a partition scheme. Third, it would intensify the internal strife between the Lebanese Forces and Walid Junblat's Progressive Socialist Party militia and further damage the national consensus. Fourth, the withdrawal would positively reinforce the Syrian position by demonstrating that time was on Syria's side and that the agreement was not the only option for withdrawals. Furthermore, Syria's indirect control of the hills overlooking Beirut would be restored through the Progressive Socialist Party. In other words, Israel was promoting a realignment of power by creating a vacuum that would surely be filled by Beirut's adversaries.

The impasse and the dilemma triggered intense diplomatic activity. Lebanese and Israeli delegations visited Washington independently in June 1983 seeking U.S. support for their respective positions, and Ambassadors Habib, Draper, and Richard Fairbanks returned to the Middle East later in the month. In the process three ideas crystallized. First, partial Israeli withdrawal should instead be a phased withdrawal in the context of a timetable for a full withdrawal. Security arrangements would be implemented as withdrawals took place. Second, a Saudi proposal was developed to the effect that the agreement be limited to security arrangements, on the basis of which simultaneous Syrian, Palestinian, and Israeli withdrawals would occur. Six months later clauses dealing with the normalization of mutual relations would be renegotiated. Third, the U.S. team explored variations on the Saudi plan in an attempt to change the relation between the agreement and the withdrawals and consequently change the time frame of the withdrawals. The proposal called for a simultaneous agreement on consecutive or rolling withdrawals, outside the context of the agreement, which would be dealt with separately after withdrawals were completed. But Israel leaked the U.S. proposals to justify rejecting them, because it insisted on simultaneous withdrawals – and partial withdrawal as the only alternative.

Diplomatic action reached its peak in July 1983 with the visits of Secretary Shultz to the Middle East and President Gemayel to Washington. Shultz's mission was to explore the circumstances under which the Syrians would leave. After visiting Lebanon, Syria, Jordan, Egypt, and Israel, he concluded that there was no substantive achievement. The talks of President Gemayel and Prime Minister Wazzan in Washington did not have any immediate impact either. A two-pronged strategy was agreed upon: the modification of Syria's position through diplomatic efforts and the exploration of variations in the mechanisms for withdrawals, and, meanwhile, the strengthening of the military and economic capabilities of Lebanon to withstand internal and external opposition.

12

Phase VI. Cease-Fire and Dialogue: Saudi-U.S. Collaboration (1983)

Saudi Arabia has consistently been a friend of Lebanon and supporter of its unity, integrity, and sovereignty. Since 1975, and particularly during the Arab initiative phase, Saudi Arabia has been involved in attempts to resolve the Lebanese crisis on the basis of three principles: preservation of Arab unity and consensus, freedom of Lebanon and all its communities, and the absolute right of the legitimate Lebanese government to decide what is best for Lebanon. Consequently, Saudi Arabia has enjoyed a unique peacemaking image within Lebanon and the Arab world.

Saudi Arabia's mediation potential became exceedingly critical for Lebanon when Syrian-Lebanese relations reached a deadlock in 1983 and the United States was not able to sustain negotiations with Syria. Both Lebanon and the United States looked to Saudi Arabia to interact with them and Syria to bridge the communication gap with Syria. Saudi Arabia wanted to work closely with the United States and Lebanon but did not want to be seen to be working openly with them for fear Syria would believe the three had ganged up against Syria. Collaborative efforts started informally between Prince Bandar bin Sultan, then Deputy National Security Adviser Robert McFarlane, and myself early in July 1983 and became visible only after McFarlane and Fairbanks were appointed special envoys to the Middle East later in the month. The United States and Saudi Arabia hoped to use their unique position and resources to influence both Israel and Syria to withdraw their forces from Lebanon on the basis of Israel's commitment to withdraw fully in the May 17 Agreement and Assad's documented commitment to the Saudis that his troops would withdraw if the Lebanese-Israeli agreement were limited to security arrangements.

Agenda for Action

The Lebanese-U.S.-Saudi collaborative efforts concentrated on three objectives: breaking the withdrawal impasse, redressing the partial Israeli withdrawal, and controlling its internal ramifications. First, in order to break the impasse, a variation on an earlier Saudi proposal was developed along the following lines: the agreement between Lebanon and Israel would be restricted to security arrangements on the basis of which simultaneous withdrawals would take place and other provisions would be negotiated later. If Gemayel, Assad, and Begin accepted this proposal, Reagan would send them letters confirming the understanding. Letters of reply would constitute an agreement, which might be concluded during a visit from Secretary Shultz. On the Arab side, the agreement would be announced at a mini-summit of Fahd, Assad, and Gemayel. When the proposal was carried independently to Damascus by Saudi and U.S. envoys, Syria's position was uncompromising on the agreement: the security arrangements as listed in the agreement were not acceptable because they imposed excessive limitations on Lebanon and dictated Lebanese-Arab relations; the agreement itself was void because it was concluded under duress; no linkage between an Israeli and an Arab presence in Lebanon could be tolerated, and, consequently, the Syrian withdrawal could be discussed only after a total Israeli withdrawal. Damascus, however, did not close the door completely. It spoke on and off about simultaneous withdrawals if the agreement were cancelled, and at one point on August 17 Khaddam went through the exercise of discussing with Fairbanks and U.S. legal adviser Davis Robinson the legality of the agreement point by point.

Second, the Israeli partial withdrawal from the Aley-Shouf area was formally approved by the Israeli cabinet on July 20, 1983. U.S. efforts concentrated on making it a step in a complete withdrawal scheme and part of an overall strategy to obtain Syria's withdrawal. Consequently, McFarlane and Fairbanks tried to obtain from Israel a notional or target date for full withdrawals, public indication that Israel had no territorial ambitions in Lebanon, and that the forthcoming IDF redeployment was a first stage in a process of withdrawal to be carried out within the context of the agreement. Israel refused to set dates, however, but agreed to make a public statement. The statement went unnoticed when it was made by Moshe Arens during a visit to Beirut on August 16, because the visit itself became an issue and precipitated a crisis in Lebanon.

Third, the ramifications of the Israeli partial withdrawal were of the most immediate concern. The Aley-Shouf region had been the scene of intense fighting between the Lebanese Forces and the Druze Progressive Socialist Party militias, both of whom regrouped into segregated enclaves with lines of demarcation that were the site of continuous fighting. Both parties depended on Israel to maintain their strength and lines of supply. It was assumed, therefore, that Israel could, if it wished, resolve the conflict, or at least disarm both parties before its departure, especially since the military buildup occurred during the Israeli occupation when the IDF was the sole security force. An Israeli withdrawal would create a security vacuum and allow for ground offensives by both parties unless the Lebanese government could deploy its forces. In addition, the deployment of the Lebanese Armed Forces into the Aley-Shouf area would improve the security of Beirut, link it with the south to prevent partition, and improve the chances for further Israeli withdrawals, which, according to Israeli authorities, were contingent upon the per-formance of the Lebanese government in Aley and the Shouf. It was, therefore, in the national interest to secure an orderly Israeli withdrawal, an internal accord to deploy the Lebanese Armed Forces and a Syrian commitment not to interfere in the areas evacuated by Israel. Early in July, Junblat and Barri issued a joint communiqué in Damascus rejecting "Lebanese Army deployment in the Lebanese mountains in case of partial Israeli withdrawal from the region," because they considered the army sectarian and confessional. Later in mid-July Junblat warned that "if an internal Lebanese political agreement is not reached, we will regrettably be forced to resist the Lebanese army and prevent its entry into the mountain area."

The Paris Accord

The Lebanese government decided not to deploy the army in Aley and the Shouf by force but rather on the basis of an agreement with the Progressive Socialist Party and the Lebanese Forces. During the month of June, tactical discussions were conducted between some army officers and Junblat aids without tangible results. Early in August, the government decided that "if Walid Junblat is the key to such an agreement we will go to him." Upon the request of President Gemayel, King Fahd and King Hussein of Jordan used their good offices to arrange for a meeting between Junblat and myself either in Jiddah or Amman in the presence of a Saudi official and solicited Assad's commitment to facilitate the reconciliation process. Junblat was elusive and did not come to a tentatively arranged meeting in Jiddah on August 21. Earlier in the week he had not shown up for an appointment with a ministerial delegation at President Franjieh's residence. Meanwhile the United States and France joined in the diplomatic efforts, and, as a result, a series of meetings was held in Paris from August 26 to 28 between the Lebanese government (Ambassador Faruq Abilama and myself) and the Progressive Socialist Party (Walid and Khalid Junblat, Marwan

Hamadah, and Dr. Hatoum). Israel promised the United States that it would postpone withdrawals as long as there was progress in the talks. Some of the meetings were attended by McFarlane and his associates, as well as François de Grossouvre, the French national security adviser, and Rafiq Hariri, a Saudi businessman of Lebanese origin close to King Fahd. After lengthy discussions we reached the following agreement:

Security Section

1. The state of fighting in the mountain shall be terminated, all military manifestations suppressed, and all parties shall refrain from any acts of terrorism or actions that threaten individual and collective security and shall stop all hostile propaganda campaigns.

2. All non-local armed forces shall withdraw from the region and shall be prevented from remaining in the Shouf, Aley, and Ba'abda districts.

3. All illegal barracks shall be closed.

4. Illegal mobilization of the mountain youth shall cease, and people shall be directed to join the government military service.

5. All heavy weapons shall be withdrawn from circulation awaiting their collection within the context of an overall solution that involves abolishing all militias.

6. All legal procedures against individuals with offenses of a political nature shall be suspended.

7. There shall be a commitment to release all kidnapped persons and to search diligently for the missing ones to return them to their families.

8. A joint committee shall be formed from the army, the Internal Security Forces, and representatives from the MNF, the Lebanese Forces, and the Higher Druze Community Commission to develop the details of this agreement and supervise its implementation. (This item was modified to include a provision that the mode of deployment and numbers of the Lebanese Armed Forces deployed will be coordinated with Junblat.)

9. This agreement shall be implemented by the forces of the legal authorities – the army, the Internal Security Forces – supported by the MNF. These forces will provide security in the Shouf, Aley, and Ba'abda districts.

Political Section

1. A coalition government shall be formed representing the different political trends in the country.

2. This government shall review the Lebanese-Israeli-U.S. agreement in the light of other alternatives that secure full withdrawals.

3. The government shall also launch a national dialogue to reach an accord on the different issues that confront the country.

It was also agreed that Junblat would seek the consent of Syria and his allies, and I would secure the approval of President Gemayel and the agreement of the Lebanese Forces. McFarlane would continue to delay the Israeli withdrawal, and Saudi Arabia, and possibly France, would mediate with Assad so that he would not obstruct the agreement.

The next day President Gemayel approved the agreement and the Lebanese Forces agreed to it. Meanwhile, Junblat went on to Geneva for a meeting with Khaddam. Limited fighting occurred in the southern suburbs of Beirut between the Lebanese Army and Amal, which was accompanied by shelling of Beirut and its eastern suburbs from positions in upper Metn under Syrian control. When the fighting subsided, Amal fighters spread into West Beirut and the army was heavily deployed there to restore order. On August 31, President Gemayel, in a cabinet meeting, affirmed that recent events "had increased his conviction that the best way to deal with this issue in a fundamental manner would be to embark immediately on the national dialogue for which he had called repeatedly." He then publicly invited, by name, the leaders of the different groups "to join the state in the making of the national decision that will save Lebanon."

Impact of Partial Withdrawal

Although contacts were continuing between Junblat and the
government, Israel refused to postpone its partial withdrawal
any longer and redeployed the IDF to the Awwali River from
late September 3 to early September 4. The Lebanese Army,
in the absence of an accord and due to its significant deployment in Beirut, was instructed not to enter the evacuated
areas but to restrict its deployment to the surrounding hills
to defend Beirut. As the IDF withdrawal was being completed, the Lebanese Forces decided to hold to their positions
in the upper region, although the army decision was com-
municated to them earlier, but handed over their positions
in the lower region to the Lebanese Armed Forces, which
established a line of defense around Beirut from Aley to Souk
al-Gharb to Khalde. The Progressive Socialist Party forces,
supported by PLO and PLA troops and Syrian artillery and
logistics, mounted a massive ground offensive, and, after a
three-day battle, took over the key town of Bhamdoun. The
Lebanese Forces retreated to Dayr al-Qamar with thousands
of people from Christian villages. The whole area down to the
Lebanese Armed Forces' line was taken by the Progressive
Socialist Party and, in the process, many villages were completely destroyed and their inhabitants massacred and thousands of civilians were displaced. For many days the anti-
government forces fought unsuccessfully against the army
in Souk al-Gharb to gain access to the presidential palace,
which was only a few miles away. On September 11, the U.S.
administration finally understood the reality of foreign involvement in the mountain war and the importance of Souk
al-Gharb for the protection of U.S. military and diplomatic
personnel and for the preservation of Lebanese legitimacy.
The rules of engagement for U.S. troops were consequently
modified so that the U.S. forces could, when threatened, support Lebanese Armed Forces' positions in the defense of
Beirut with air and artillery strikes, although not by ground
action. the U.S. Marine and Navy support – along with help
from the meager Lebanese Air Force for the first time on

September 16 – held the Lebanese Army together as it defended its lines under highly unfavorable conditions against the Progressive Socialist Party and its allies in the mountains and against Amal south of Beirut.

Negotiations for a Cease-fire

When the fighting started, the Saudi envoys Prince Bandar and Rafiq Hariri and the U.S. envoys McFarlane and Fairbanks worked closely with us literally around the clock to secure a cease-fire. The first proposal was formulated immediately after the fighting broke out, between Bandar, Assad, Khaddam, and Junblat. When Bandar went back to Damascus on September 5 with the approval of all parties to the cease-fire proposal, he was surprised by Syria's rejection because Syria now believed the facts on the ground had been changed. Consequently, an emergency meeting of the Saudi cabinet was held on September 7 and a statement was issued expressing regret that Saudi Arabia's "mediation efforts had failed to achieve results, and therefore it found itself obliged to freeze its efforts until encouraging positive signs appeared, which could justify the resumption of these efforts."

The next day President Assad asked King Fahd to resume the Saudi mediation, and the Saudi, U.S., and Lebanese teams met in Larnaca, Cyprus on September 9 and drafted a cease-fire proposal that emphasized the right of the Lebanese state to extend its sovereignty over all of Lebanon through the deployment of the Lebanese Army and internal security forces, a cease-fire over the entire Lebanese territory, security arrangements in the Shouf and Aley to make the cease-fire hold, and a call for immediate and comprehensive national dialogue in the presence of Saudi and Syrian observers.

For the next two weeks discussions centered around the conditions for a cease-fire as they related to three issues: the role of the army, the participants in a national dialogue, and the venue for the meeting. The opposition, backed by Syria, insisted that the army should not be involved in internal matters and should be withdrawn from the lines it was then holding. The government position was that the Lebanese law stipulated the conditions under which the cabinet could use the army for internal security purposes. Moreover, a cease-fire without the extension of state authority would create only a special status buffer zone, which would cut central Lebanon from the south. As to participation in a national dialogue, the government suggested the inclusion of all major political leaders, while Syria objected to the participation of the prime minister, the speaker of the parliament, and some other leaders. The venue for the meeting fluctuated among more than 10 alternatives, while the government's preference was for the presidential palace or Saudi Arabia. After frantic shuttling between Beirut, Larnaca, Jiddah, and Damascus, a cease-fire agreement was finally reached and made effective on 6 a.m. September 26. The terms of the agreement were as follows:

1. An immediate cease-fire throughout Lebanese territory and on all axes and points of contact. Neutral observers shall supervise the cease-fire in the areas of fighting.
Facilitation of the return to their homes of Lebanese who had been forced to flee from 1975 to the present, as well as of arrangements for relief operations.
2. A committee of the following parties is formed:
− the army
− the Lebanese Front
− the National Salvation Front
− the Amal Movement
to establish the arrangements for the cease-fire and its consolidation.
3. The president of the republic calls an urgent and comprehensive meeting to begin the national dialogue immediately. The meeting brings together:
− The National Salvation Front (Messrs. Suleiman Franjieh, Rashid Karami, Walid Junblat)

— The Lebanese Front (Messrs. Camille Chamoun, Pierre Gemayel)

— The Amal Movement (Mr. Nabih Barri)

— Messrs. Sa'ib Salam, Adel Usayran, and Raymond Edde.

4. The president of the republic is pleased to welcome the attendance of a delegate from fraternal Saudi Arabia and a delegate from fraternal Syria.

It was also agreed that the meeting would take place in Saudi Arabia and that the official Lebanese delegation would include members from the legislative and executive branches.

The security committee was formed immediately and started its meetings with the active involvement of Rafiq Hariri. The notion of neutral observers could not be implemented because Syria rejected the concept of UN observers on domestic cease-fire lines, and the different parties could not agree on the nationality of non-UN observers. The national dialogue meeting was delayed because the place of the meeting became an issue again. Syria was not keen on having the meeting in Saudi Arabia, and the opposition refused to have it held at the presidential palace in Ba'abda. Other places in Lebanon proved unsafe for one party or another. Finally, on October 21, all participants agreed, with the Swiss government's consent, to hold the talks in Geneva on October 31, 1983.

13

Phase VII. Dialogue I:
The Lebanese Initiative
(October–November 1983)

The framework for national dialogue was formulated by a committee representing all the participants named in the cease-fire agreement except Edde, who declined the invitation. On October 13, 1983, the committee unanimously proposed the following agenda:

1. A comprehensive and lasting national accord;
2. The identity of Lebanon and its Arab and international relations;
3. The termination of Israeli occupation;
4. The withdrawal of all non-Lebanese forces from Lebanon except those present with government consent;
5. Political, social, economic, administrative, educational, financial, and communication reforms;
6. The provision of social justice, equality, and equal opportunities among all Lebanese and fulfillment of a balanced integrated development for all Lebanese regions;
7. A discussion of the conditions of the military establishment;
8. The extension of the sovereignty of the state over all Lebanese territory.

The dialogue talks opened in Geneva on October 31 on schedule after resolving last minute difficulties related to seating arrangements and protocol.[15] Initially, the atmosphere was highly charged with tension, hostility, accusations, and plain apprehension as a result of years of conflict, separation, and bitter experiences. But there was also an awareness of the historic opportunity and of the great expectations and high hopes of Lebanon's people and friends. In his opening address, President Gemayel tried to set the conciliatory tone of the conference:

> We all bear our share of the responsibility. Whoever among us is without sin or fault, let him throw the first stone. We came here to save Lebanon, to unite its people, to restore its sovereignty, and to strengthen the brotherly bonds among the Lebanese and with their Arab brothers on the basis of justice and dignity.

As the conference progressed, a momentum for the relaxation of tension and understanding developed. The official meetings were characterized by an unusually nonconfrontational manner and genuine attempts at accommodation, compromise, and the exploration of solutions. The side meetings also witnessed reconciliations and a renewal of relations. In the process, Gemayel's presidency was reaffirmed and given a vote of confidence.

Saudi Arabia, in the person of Minister of State Muhammad Mas'ud, played the official role of an observer who would not "be an obstacle for whatever the conference agrees upon for Lebanon's welfare within its Arab framework, accords, and commitments," and the unofficial role of a dynamic facilitator in the person of Rafiq Hariri. Syria, represented by Foreign Minister Khaddam, did not pretend to be a neutral observer, but announced its agenda forcefully from the beginning: (1) decoupling and differentiation between the Syrian and Israeli presence in, and withdrawal from, Lebanon. "Those who want to equate Syria and Israel," Khaddam declared, "cannot do so. Anyone who considers Syria like Israel is mistaken"; (2) opposition to the Israeli occupation and cancellation of the May 17 Agreement. Only three days earlier, a Gemayel-Assad summit had been postponed because Gemayel had resisted Syria's insistence on making a negative a priori decision on the agreement before the visit and the Geneva talks. The United States was equally interested in the proceedings of the conference. Its team, headed by Richard Fairbanks, held intensive informal talks with all the participants to assist in the reconciliation process and to find a solution to the "May 17" impasse. These goals, if achieved, would spare the United States further military involvement and create suitable conditions for its own withdrawal, especially after the agony and controversy created by the bombing of the marine headquarters in Beirut a week earlier.

Although the agenda was presumably set by the preparatory committee, the conference had to deal with priorities and sequence, particularly between the two issues of liberation and reform. The Lebanese Front, sensing a divergence of opinion on the withdrawal issues including the fate of the May 17 Agreement, preferred to start with this for two reasons. First it would be better for Lebanon's image to have disagreement on external rather than internal matters, and, second, there was no point, in the absence of a full agreement, in making internal concessions that might become a bench mark for future negotiation. Similarly, the opposition National Salvation Front wanted to start with the external issues, but for a different reason. To them, the agreement was a critical national issue, the resolution of which was a prerequisite for the resumption of the political process. Moreover, both the National Salvation Front and moderate Muslim participants considered that a resolution of the identity issue would clarify Lebanon's position in the Arab-Israeli conflict and establish the logical rationale for the negative attitude that the conference would naturally take toward the agreement. There was also a general perception that liberation required national unity, and that unity could only be built on a common acceptance of a set of principles, the most essential of which was Lebanon's identity.

For all of the reasons given above, every group believed the Lebanese identity issue must be resolved at the state level as an issue that would unite, rather than a community or individual issue that would divide. This agreement reflected a conscious unwillingness to address the communal identity issues discussed in chapter 2 on the bases both that resolution was not practicable in the near term and that state identity rendered the other levels moot in terms of the Lebanese conflict. Consequently, the agenda was established in the following sequence: identity, withdrawals, and internal reform.

Lebanon's Identity

There was a consensus on Lebanon's independence, unity, and territorial integrity, as well as a rejection of any partition or the annexation of all or parts of Lebanon to its neighbors. The question was then the identity of the entity called Lebanon. Participants approached the issue from four perspectives. Camille Chamoun tried to avoid any anthropological discussion of the identity of the Lebanese people because of the ethnically pluralistic nature of the Lebanese society. Instead, he tried to focus on the identity of the state and define it in terms of Lebanon's membership in the Arab League, which did not necessarily make the Lebanese any more Arab than the people of Somalia, Djibouti, or Mauritania. Pierre Gemayel at first considered the discussion of Lebanon's Arab identity an unnecessary exercise because it should have been taken for granted (just as no one argues whether France is European) and put Lebanon on the defensive to prove its affiliation. He then distinguished, like Chamoun, between "political" and "real" identity. Politically, Lebanon had launched the concept of Arab nationalism as a secular notion but, unfortunately, the other Arab states had superimposed a religious dimension upon it. The "real" identity could only be determined on the basis of research in anthropology, history, and geography. To Gemayel, Lebanon's distinctive identification was twofold: as a neutral between East and West, according to the spirit of the 1943 National Pact, and as possessing the freedom wherein, unlike in other Arab states, Christians and Muslims could be themselves and feel they were in their own country. On the other side, Sa'ib Salam tried to define Lebanon's Arab identity within the context of the "finality" of the Lebanese identity. In other words, Lebanon's Arab affiliation neither made the Lebanese entity transitory and part of a whole nor artificial within its present boundaries. On the contrary, Lebanon rested its relations with its fraternal Arab states "on brotherhood, cooperation, and mutual respect for the independence of each state and its sovereignty over its territory . . . and noninterference of any state in the internal affairs of the others." Rashid Karami insisted on an operational definition of the Arab identity to avoid ambiguity and the passing on of a time bomb to the next government of national unity. He therefore demanded that Lebanon's Arab affiliation be reflected "in all political, cultural, economic, social, informational, educational, and defense domains."

After lengthy discussions the conference adopted the following resolution:

> Lebanon is a sovereign, free, independent country, united in its territory, people, and institutions within its borders as defined in the Lebanese constitution and recognized internationally. Lebanon is of Arab affiliation and identity, a founding and active member of the Arab League, and is committed to all its charters. The state shall embody these principles in all fields without exception.

The Fate of the May 17 Agreement

The discussion of this item started with two diametrically opposed positions. On one side, the agreement was thought to be a viable mechanism for securing an Israeli withdrawal.

If Syria was made to agree to withdraw, there would be two withdrawals, Syrian and Israeli. On the other side, the agreement was considered a nonstarter because it contradicted Lebanon's identity and sovereignty and should not have been concluded with the enemy.

The conference quickly realized that a crisis situation was developing whereby all paths lead to dead-ends. It did not take much to realize that the agreement was not implementable: if ratified, Syria would not withdraw, nor then would Israel; if abrogated, Israel would not withdraw, nor then would Syria. The problem became that of damage control, and two options were immediately dismissed. Ratification could not be considered because of the lack of national consensus and the effect on withdrawal. Outright abrogation would antagonize the United States, which was a party to the agreement, diminish Lebanon's credibility in the international world, and create a dangerous precedent regarding the continuity of the legitimacy of the Lebanese government and its constitutional institutions and processes. The only other option left for consideration was the freezing of the agreement.

Although the agreement was, for all practical purposes, frozen by the government, an official freezing, in Nabih Barri's view, was dangerous for three reasons: (1) the occupation would continue, (2) the initiative on the fate of the agreement would be taken from the hands of the government, and (3) the government could not follow other channels in pursuit of liberation, such as the security council. There was also some diversity on the purpose of the freezing. Chamoun proposed freezing the agreement until a government of national unity was formed, which could then "thaw" the agreement, review it, and decide its fate. Karami suggested freezing with the intention of abrogating it when the appropriate time and conditions were reached. Franjieh thought of freezing as a mechanism to give the president time to consult with the United States.

In the process, a consensus developed that further exploration was needed by the president – but with two different sets of boundary conditions. One group wanted to leave to the president the freedom to explore all avenues to secure Israel's withdrawal and Lebanon's sovereignty, while the other group wanted an implied understanding on the abrogation of the May 17 Agreement and would then leave to the president the time and style of abrogation in consultation with the United States and through constitutional channels.

It was finally agreed that President Gemayel would consult with President Reagan and the fate of the agreement would be decided upon his return and in consultation with Syria. There were, however, different conceptions of the message that should be carried to Reagan. While President Gemayel wanted tactically to ask Reagan to deliver the goods, that is, withdrawals, or cancel the agreement, the National Salvation Front wanted Gemayel to ask for its abrogation. Syrian Foreign Minister Khaddam believed that Israel would be willing to withdraw without a Syrian and Palestinian withdrawal only if the agreement were ratified. Therefore he wanted Gemayel to request from Reagan the abrogation of the agreement, while Syria would be ready to negotiate for security arrangements. The final resolution of the conference gave Gemayel the necessary margin of maneuverability:

> The conferees asked President Gemayel to carry out the necessary international measures and contacts to end the Israeli occupation and to ensure Lebanon's full and absolute sovereignty over all its territory.

Internal Reform

There was no interest in pursuing any discussion of internal political and social reforms before Gemayel's meeting with President Reagan. Participants submitted their proposals, however, and their advisers (except for Nabih Barri's) stayed behind for one week and studied, as a committee, all the proposals. The committee made a comparative analysis of topics showing areas and degrees of agreement, to be submitted to a second conference. It is worth noting that the areas of general agreement did not deviate significantly from the spirit and content of the "constitutional document" announced by Franjieh in 1976.

14

Phase VIII. Between Dialogues (November 1983–March 1984)

The national dialogue conference was adjourned on November 4, 1983 until after Gemayel's meeting with Reagan, which was set for December 3. All parties used this waiting period to consolidate their positions. Internally, the opposition to the government kept up the pressure by reiterating its demand for the abrogation of the May 17 Agreement, keeping the tension on the cease-fire lines in Aley and Beirut and escalating the shelling of Beirut and the surrounding areas. At the same time, the Lebanese Forces called for the ratification of the agreement and 37 members of Parliament, including the speaker, issued a communiqué indicating their refusal to abrogate or freeze the agreement as long as no other solution for securing Israel's withdrawal had been found. Externally, Israel warned that "the cancellation of the agreement meant the cancellation of Lebanon's independence," and sealed the south except for the two passages over the Awwali bridges that were opened intermittently. Syria in turn held its position, awaiting the results of Gemayel's Washington visit. A Gemayel-Assad summit scheduled for November 14 was postponed due to Assad's sudden illness, and, instead, Khaddam visited Beirut to dispel any political interpretation about the postponement of the summit and to affirm Syria's support for Gemayel's trip. Meanwhile, the new U.S. envoy to the Middle East, former Secretary of Defense Donald Rumsfeld, visited the area to explore new ideas and alternatives in preparation for the Washington meeting.

Gemayel's trip to Washington occurred under unfavorable conditions. The pressure was mounting on the U.S. administration by Congress and the public to disengage from Lebanon, and United States-Israeli relations were at their best after a "successful" visit by Yitzhak Shamir and Moshe Arens. Syria, meanwhile, was perceived as the problem that was obstructing the withdrawal process, and the United States was therefore not willing to grant it any victory no matter how small. Moreover, the United States was not ready to pressure Israel for any concessions before seeing positive signs from Syria. As a result, the United States was in no mood to support an abrogation of the May 17 Agreement. Instead, it reaffirmed its commitment to the more comprehensive objective of restoring Lebanese sovereignty by securing the withdrawal of both Syrian and Israeli forces, helping the Lebanese government consolidate its authority in the unoccupied territories and restore civil authorities in occupied areas, and supporting the Lebanese Armed Forces with arms and training to replace the MNF. The United States was anxious to solve its own problem in Lebanon as well and therefore attached great importance to the reconciliation process. In short, President Gemayel could not secure Washington's consent for the abrogation of the agreement.

The results were not satisfactory to the opposition and Syria. The security situation deteriorated and political tensions mounted again. Mediation efforts by Franjieh kept the situation from escalating beyond control, and Saudi efforts materialized in tripartite meetings of the Lebanese, Syrian, and Saudi foreign ministers. Despite these efforts, Lebanon, once again, found itself at an impasse. The security plans could not get off the ground, and the political process reached a deadlock. Syria and the opposition refused to join any further national dialogue before the May 17 Agreement was abrogated. Meanwhile Prime Minister Wazzan's cabinet resigned and, under the circumstances, no broad-based government could be formed. On the other hand, an abrogation of the agreement did not have enough support from the Lebanese Christians and the United States, and would obstruct any chances for an Israeli withdrawal.

In an attempt to resolve the deadlock, the Lebanese-U.S. consultations continued seeking a formula, independent of the May 17 Agreement, that would satisfy both Israel and Syria and make them withdraw from Lebanon. The United States maintained that it would not endorse an abrogation of the agreement but would continue to support Lebanon and pursue a policy of seeking withdrawals even if Lebanon were to abrogate the agreement. On February 5, 1984, Gemayel tried to revive the political process by announcing in an address to the nation an open-ended policy comprising (1) a detailed program of political and social reform, (2) an invitation for the resumption of national dialogue with no preconditions or a priori positions, (3) the beginning of consultations to form a national unity government, (4) the readiness of the Lebanese Armed Forces to be deployed on the coastal road in unoccupied Christian and Druze areas, (5) the strengthening of Lebanese-Syrian negotiations to reach a formula that would allow Lebanon to deploy its forces in Syrian-controlled areas, and (6) an acknowledgment of the need to seek a substitute for the May 17 Agreement—a formula that would guarantee full withdrawals.

In spite of Gemayel's proposals, the situation deteriorated in West Beirut the next day and Amal all but took control of that part of the city as the green line between East and West Beirut was reinstituted. The same day, Reagan authorized the U.S. naval forces to retaliate against any units firing into Greater Beirut from Syrian-controlled areas as well as against any units directly attacking U.S. personnel, which resulted in an escalation of U.S. military involvement. At the same time, Reagan announced his intention of shortly redeploying the marines to the ships in stages in response to the United States domestic mood in an election year and to the climate in Congress after retired Admiral Robert Clarence Long's Commission report on the bombing of marine headquarters in Beirut.

Still further attempts were pursued to resolve the crisis. Former President Franjieh suggested that Gemayel send a letter to Assad committing himself to the abrogation of the agreement by a majority vote of the national dialogue conference. Meanwhile Saudi Arabia and Lebanon collaborated on a draft package deal that included the following elements: (1) an abrogation of the May 17 Agreement, (2) security arrangements acceptable to Israel, (3) an agreement on internal reforms, (4) an agreement with Syria to withdraw from Lebanon, (5) an endorsement of the concept of simultaneous withdrawals to commence not later than three months from the time security arrangements were agreed upon, and (6) formation of a national unity government. Lebanon tended to favor the Saudi formula because it was a package deal that addressed the withdrawal issue and preserved the credibility of the government.

As both plans were being negotiated, the situation deteriorated further in the Aley region, as a result of which the Lebanese Army withdrew on February 14 and the Progressive Socialist Party took control of the west ridge and connected with West Beirut, posing a military threat to the presidential palace in Ba'abda and to East Beirut and its surroundings. From then on, the situation worsened. Syria rejected the Saudi package deal, insisting on unconditional abrogation of the agreement. No government could be formed. U.S. gunfire proved insufficient, and the U.S. special initiative was practically terminated, while the areas under government control were shelled continuously and threatened by a ground offensive.

On February 23, 1984 President Gemayel made the difficult decision to abrogate the May 17 Agreement. The rationale, as he articulated later, was as follows: "When negotiating with Israel with the participation of the United States was the only imperative option to regain the land, we did not hesitate before this option, and when the abrogation of the May 17 Agreement became the only imperative option to unite the people we did not hesitate to abrogate."[16] On February 29, Gemayel and Assad met in Damascus to initiate a new phase of relations and work out the details of the abrogation process. On March 5, a revived Lebanese cabinet took the necessary constitutional step to put an end to the saga of the May 17 Agreement with two complementary decisions:

1. To abrogate the unratified May 17 Agreement, considering it null and void, and to cancel anything that could have resulted from it;

2. To take necessary steps by the government to lead to the formulation of security arrangements and measures that provide sovereignty and stability in southern Lebanon, prevent infiltration across the southern borders, and secure the withdrawal of all Israeli forces from all the Lebanese territory.

The security situation improved immediately. Political life was resumed, and the second round of national dialogue was set for March 12 in Lausanne, Switzerland.

15

Phase IX. Dialogue II: A Formula for a New Lebanon (March 1984)

The second national dialogue conference in Lausanne [17] from March 12-20, 1984 was restricted to those who were involved in the Geneva round, although there were attempts up to the last minute to include representatives of the Greek Orthodox, Greek Catholic, and Armenian communities. The Lausanne talks were, however, conducted under a new set of conditions. What was perceived as a "U.S. option" or an "Israeli option" had failed, and the "Syrian option" had just prevailed. Khaddam joined the conference in a different capacity — not only as a newly appointed vice president of Syria but also as a representative of a country with no enemies among the participating parties and no vital demands to push for. Both the National Salvation Front and President Gemayel were expecting to be rewarded by Syria, the first for opposing the May 17 Agreement and the second for abrogating it. Syria, therefore, found itself in a delicate position: it could not withdraw its support of the front or pressure it to give up its internal demands, nor could it pressure Gemayel for further concessions or compromises. At the same time, the conference was a test for the credibility and efficacy of the "Syrian option."

Syria's earlier success was the second conference's weakness, as the Syrian option became a target for obstruction and sabotage by all parties that wanted to deprive Damascus of the fruits of its success. The "timely" renewal of fierce fighting on all fronts in and around Beirut and the relentless shelling was interpreted by Khaddam as an attempt to blackmail Syria. Consequently, Khaddam's tactics seemed to fluctuate between two extremes: heavy handed pressure to make the conference succeed and a hands-off posture to avoid bearing the consequences should it fail. On one hand, Khaddam delivered an ultimatum to the participants: the region could no longer bear the conflict in Lebanon and, therefore, the conferees could not leave without an agreement no matter how long it took, otherwise Syria would look for solutions and impose them on Lebanon. On the other hand, Khaddam tried not to be caught in the cross fire of proposals and counterproposals, and at one point he reacted disproportionately to a mild Lebanese Forces communiqué criticizing his involvement in the talks so that he could get out of the task of synthesizing and compromising the conflicting demands of the different parties – although he was finally dragged in.

Saudi Arabia took its usual dual position by being an officially passive observer (Mas'ud) and an unofficially active, sometimes aggressive, mediator (Hariri). The Saudi team stressed the importance of "putting the Lebanese house in order" through national reconciliation and unity. Hariri actively tried to break deadlocks and broker pragmatic compromises, but was faced with historical prejudices and communal stubbornness.

Agenda of the Conference and the Conferees

The sole item of the agenda was the reformation of the political system and the development of a political structure or formula suitable for a new Lebanon. The question was, as Gemayel put it in his opening address, "whether Lebanon after the years of war will return to what it was in terms of constitutional powers, political practices, and military, social, economic, administrative, and cultural institutions. Will Lebanon be the first venture of the 1940s [referring to the 1943 National Pact] or will there be another venture in the 1980s derived from a historic accord among the Lebanese?"

All the conferees approached this question not from an ideological perspective but rather from a purely communal one. The Maronites and the Sunnis, the major beneficiaries of the National Pact, currently had unfavorable positions on the ground after the fighting in Lebanon and considered that, unless they played it well, any modifications in the system would be at their expense. The Lebanese Front, however, applied the tactic of running forward and took the initiative in proposing a radical change (federation) that would guarantee them a degree of autonomy. The Sunnis tried to turn their demands, such as the powers of the prime minister, into a wider Muslim demand. The Druze had won on the ground beyond their numbers, and, therefore, were looking for a formula, not based on numbers, that would give them a better share, such as a senate or a decentralization scheme. The Shi'a, also winners, considered themselves entitled to a bigger share in a new Lebanon, especially because they considered themselves the largest community although the least privileged and represented. Therefore, unlike their Druze allies, they considered a simple numerical democracy would be in their favor.

It was evident that the ideological polarization created by the May 17 Agreement and the identity issue was superficial and it soon disappeared, to be replaced by a deeper and stronger polarization along religious lines. The mixed National Salvation Front disintegrated, and conferees regrouped into confessional clusters. The unfortunate reconfiguration tainted the otherwise progressive proposals of secularization and politicosocial reforms with confessional overtones and moved the dialogue from a constructive debate on the best structure to rebuild Lebanon into a more sensitive and charged zero-sum game among the different communities. Under the circumstances, Gemayel had to struggle to maintain his role as arbitrator. Moreover, Khaddam's role was diffused as he found himself in an unenviable no-win position whereby any move could be interpreted for or against one community or another.

In spite of these differences, there was a consensus on the finality of Lebanon as an entity and its general political framework: a democratic parliamentary republic open to the world and built on the foundations of human rights, equity, justice, and freedom. There was also a strong conviction that the 1943 National Pact, in its present form, was no longer satisfactory in light of the new political and demographic developments. The alternatives explored covered a wide spectrum ranging from federalism, based on a pluralistic notion of Lebanon, and nonconfessionalism, derived from a unitarian view of Lebanon.

Federalism and Plurality

The Lebanese Front represented by Camille Chamoun and Pierre Gemayel called for a federal system whereby Lebanon would be a united republic composed of states with no boundary restrictions between them and in which the federal government handled foreign affairs, monetary affairs, defense, civic and real estate laws, and overall development, while the state authorities handle everything else. The proposal was based on the following premises: (1) Lebanon was comprised of diverse religious and cultural communities each having its own character and history; (2) the present Lebanese state, which was unitary, was appropriate for a homogeneous society, while Lebanese society was diverse and pluralistic; (3) confessional diversity should be cherished and respected, unlike the policy of the present system, which vacillated between suppressing and preserving it; (4) confessional coexistence should be comprehensive; (5) federation was a viable alternative to partition and a unifying force because it would prevent confessional friction; and (6) decentralization would promote the development of local life in all areas and would lead to prosperity in underdeveloped areas.

Pluralism has been an essential element in recent Lebanese Christian political thinking and a defense mechanism against the possibility of becoming a marginalized minority. The Lebanese Front, as early as January 1977, when Suleiman Franjieh was still a member, adopted the notion that the pluralistic nature of Lebanese society should be a basis

> for the political structure of a united Lebanon . . . and a mechanism to prevent conflict between the Lebanese. . . . each cultural community will handle its own affairs, particularly those related to liberty, culture, education, finance, security, social justice, and foreign cultural and spiritual relations, according to its own choices.

The same basic philosophy was reiterated in a 1980 statement in which the Lebanese Front said it was necessary to reassess the 1943 formula:

> This may require evolving the formula into some kind of decentralization, federation, or confederation within the framework of a united Lebanon to divert future tragedies of the type that have befallen Lebanon since 1840.

The Lebanese Front considered the status of minorities the key to the Lebanese conflict, because real peace could only be achieved if each community had freedom, security, and sovereignty over its fate. In this regard "the Christian community does not want for itself more than for others, nor will it accept less than what others want." The Council of Catholic Patriarchs and Bishops supported the same view in a December 1983 statement, asserting that

> the appropriate basis for democracy is not numbers but rather the ability to allow individuals and communities in the same country to express and realize their personalities and special characteristics, without having a majority dominate a minority or a minority exploit a majority. . . . This may be facilitated by adopting administrative-developmental decentralization.

The conference did not take the federalism concept seriously, and there was no systematic discussion of its premises and the implications of implementing it. Franjieh dismissed it quickly as an untimely and inappropriate move because Lebanon, coming out of a war, needed mechanisms to unify the country. Rashid Karami questioned the feasibility of the idea considering the incongruence between demographic clusters and geographic distribution. Khaddam raised the issue that pluralism contradicted the decision taken in Geneva regarding the Arab identity of Lebanon, because one could not be an Arab and at the same time consider one's culture Maronite or Sunni or Orthodox. Sa'ib Salam also rejected pluralism, asserting the unitarian nature of Lebanon by virtue of its language and geography. Only Junblat, as a Druze, did not condemn the proposal. In fact, when the conference became highly polarized, Junblat declared that, as a Druze, he wanted nothing, but "if necessary" he added, "I want to go back and discuss the proposal of the Lebanese Front, which is federalism . . . . It is a good idea."

Nonconfessionalism and Unitariness

Nabih Barri, and later on the Muslim participants in a joint statement, called for the abolition of "political confessionalism." Political and administrative positions would no longer be assigned according to a confessional quota or affiliation. "Religious confessionalism," however, in contrast to secularism, would be retained in that the private affairs of individuals (such as marriage and inheritance) would continue to be governed and conducted by religious laws, personnel, and judiciary systems. The proposal was accompanied by three restrictive elements: the creation of a senate in which the major religious communities would be equally represented, the abolition of confessionalism from civil service only after the rights of the underrepresented communities were met, and a shift in powers from the president to the prime minister. The proposal was based on the following premises: (1) Lebanese society is unitary and, therefore, members of different communities should be treated equally and on the basis of merit rather than confessional affiliation; (2) political confessionalism, according to Article 95 of the Constitution, is transitory and must be abolished; and (3) political confessionalism, as reflected by the election system, tends to favor extremist leaders from both groups who play on Christian fears and the Muslims' sense of deprivation, while a nonconfessional system of election would favor moderates.

The abolition of confessionalism has been a component of the platform of ideological parties such as the Progressive Socialist Party, the Syrian Social National Party, and the Communist organizations as a mechanism to break into the system – as well as an essential element in recent mainstream Islamic political thinking as a mechanism to redress a perceived discrimination against them. (Full secularization has been advocated by a minority of Christian and Muslim elites.) As early as August 1975, the Program of National and Progressive Forces (later known as the Lebanese National Movement), centered on the abolition of confessionalism as a system of privileges and the institution of a new election system that would treat Lebanon as one electorate unit and would be based on proportional representation. These "Forces" considered the abolition of confessionalism from public representation as a first step toward its elimination from all texts and from the political life in Lebanon, which was one of the most essential objectives of their struggle. In what seemed nonsequential, the program called for a transfer of power from the president to the prime minister whereby the prime minister would be elected by parliament, form the cabinet, lead discussion in cabinet meetings, and preside over meetings of ministers. If the president did not sign a decree, the prime minister could issue it after a specified period.

In September 1983, Muslim political and religious leaders articulated in a comprehensive statement of "Basic Principles" the general feeling, developed over the past years, that Muslims have been marginalized "as a result of the confessional policies, positions, and practices that have marked

Lebanese public life since independence." They called for "an abolition of political confessionalism from all state functions and institutions" and asserted their rejection of any kind of political decentralization. Meanwhile, they called for the realization and strengthening of the genuine national entity through which "the entity of each Lebanese group would be realized in accordance with the principles of justice and equality, so that the entity of no one group would be dissolved or distorted for the sake of the artificial gigantism of another entity."

The concept of nonconfessionalism was rejected as quickly as the concept of federalism, on four grounds. First, it seemed ironic that nonconfessionalism was presented as a confessional demand within a package that aimed for confessional gain in the form of the creation of a senate (to give the Druze a presidency), the transfer of certain powers from the president to the Sunni prime minister, and the realization of more representation for the Shi'a on the basis of their numerical size. Second, the Christians argued that the whole notion was unrealistic because nonconfessionalism would be nominal because of the intense religious feelings on both sides and the Islamic theological position against full secularism. Therefore, the political system should reflect the reality of confessionalism in a positive manner. Third, as a derivate of the earlier point, Christians found nonconfessionalism threatening to their freedom. They agreed that the rule of numerical majority should apply only when the majority was political and could be joined by any citizen. In Lebanon the majority is confessional and static; there is no crossing of lines. In this case, the freedom of minorities could only be guaranteed by a structural power-sharing formula, otherwise, one community, by a simple majority, could have a monopoly over all powers and dominate other communities. Christians also wondered how numerical democracy had become desirable only when Muslims thought they attained it, while, when Christians were a clear majority, sharing of power was the desirable principle. Finally, the abolition of confessionalism, and consequently the quota system, would transform high level appointments from intracommunal to intercommunal struggle and plague the system with a continuous built-in crisis.

The Compromise Paper

In an attempt to bridge the gap between the two extreme positions of federalism and nonconfessionalism, the secretariat of the conference submitted a working paper based on three premises. First, neither federalism nor confessionalism could attract enough support to be adopted. Therefore, a middle ground must be sought. Second, the areas of agreement identified by the Committee of Advisers immediately following the Geneva talks could serve as a core around which to build. Third, at this abnormal point in Lebanon's national life, it was neither desirable nor feasible to make a final decision regarding the formalization or abolition of confessionalism. What was needed was an agreement on a system that would be flexible and sensitive to future trends, so that, if communal feelings were to subside, the system could evolve smoothly into less confessionalism, and, if communal feelings were to intensify, the system could evolve as smoothly into more decentralization. The paper was structured around two concepts:

1. Political centralization that guaranteed unity of land, people, and institutions, national balance, and equality among communities;
2. Wide administrative decentralization that allowed people to participate directly in the development of all regions equitably and comprehensively.

At the central level, the paper advocated the following measures to improve participation in government and public administration: (1) the distribution of present and additionally created high level posts among the major communities; (2) the reform of the electorate system to increase the number of representatives and allocate them equally between Christians and Muslims; (3) the creation of a socioeconomic council composed of representatives from different economic, social, cultural, and scientific groups; and (4) improvement in the status of the prime minister by having him nominated by parliament, form a cabinet jointly with the president, and countersign all decrees, which was basically a formalization of the present practice. To strengthen administrative decentralization, the paper recommended the strengthening of local authorities, the creation of district councils by election, and the delegation of authority by central agencies to local branches. Finally, nonconfessionalism would be approached in an evolving and phased manner starting with the abolition of confessional criteria in appointments below Category 1 in the civil service, which would be divided equally between Christians and Muslims; the elimination of any reference to religious affiliation on identification cards; and the penalization of instigators of religious conflicts.

The secretariat's paper was not endorsed by the Lebanese Front and was criticized by the Muslim leaders. Rashid Karami considered the paper too general to pass a judgment on and sought clarification on the powers of the prime minister. Both Nabih Barri and Sa'ib Salam insisted on the abolition of political confessionalism. Walid Junblat regarded the paper as too traditional and unrepresentative of his views and those of the Lebanese Front, both of which called for a radical constitutional change. This paper, he said, "gives the impression that we came here to become ministers, or speakers of parliament, or vice prime ministers. My people will kill me — we came for something more radical." On the substantive side, there was strong disagreement on the extent of decentralization and the division of authority between the president and the prime minister. Although administrative decentralization was accepted by all, developmental decentralization was rejected by Barri, for fear of locking the underdeveloped regions, which are predominantly Shi'a, into a permanent state of poverty. Moreover, there was confusion between the notion of decentralization whereby decisions would be made centrally and implemented locally and the notion of local authorities based on the participation of people in the decisions and the management of their affairs. Disagreements on power distribution centered on who would appoint the prime minister – the president or the parliament – and who would form the cabinet and who would preside over it.

The conference, reaching a deadlock, turned to Khaddam, in collaboration with the Saudi team, to try to narrow differences and produce a compromise position that could be adopted by the conference.

'Abd al-Halim Khaddam's Paper

After a full day of intensive discussions, Khaddam drafted a document that was ideologically consistent with the 1943 National Pact and the secretariat's paper. It represented a modified and tightened version of a balanced confessional system, based on the rationale that one could not jump directly into radical reform, certainly not with the Lausanne conferees who were part of the old system. So the objective of the paper was to "delineate the responsibilities of the president, the prime minister, and the cabinet and to institutionalize the oral tradition . . . so that government style would not depend on personal character." Khaddam focused on the following basic ideas:

1. The abolition of confessionalism in the civil service except in Category 1 positions, which would be assigned equally and alternately to Muslims and Christians;
2. The designation of the cabinet as the highest executive and administrative authority, institutionalizing its powers;
3. The shifting of certain powers from president to prime minister (along the lines proposed in the Islamic paper);
4. The distribution of parliamentary seats equally between Christians and Muslims;

5. An administrative decentralization (along lines proposed in the secretariat's paper);

6. Economic, social, and education reforms.

The Christians saw three major problems with the paper. First, it rewarded the Sunni community by strengthening the status of the prime minister and ignored the demands of the two communities that were problematic, namely, the Druze and the Shi'a. It was, therefore, theorized that the Sunni share in power was institutionalized under Saudi pressure and taken out of the game, so that, in a second round of bargaining, the Shi'a and Druze communities would demand their share at the expense of the Christians. Second, the paper, in shifting power from the president to the prime minister, was disturbing the internal equilibrium and giving power to one community at the expense of another. Third, the distribution of the president's powers among the different confessional groups in the cabinet would weaken the presidency as a symbol of national unity and leadership and legitimize the intercommunal power struggle at the highest level. This approach would turn the political system, after it turned the civil service, into a profit-making partnership, each partner seeking quick dividends rather than long-term investment.

Unexpectedly, it was Franjieh, Syria's friend, who blocked Khaddam's paper. Franjieh first asserted his credentials as a good Lebanese Arab by insisting on labeling Israel an enemy in any conference reference and on issuing a one-month ultimatum to the United States to force the Israelis to withdraw from Lebanon or else the Lebanese government would break its diplomatic relations with the United States. He then, as a good Lebanese Maronite, declared his unwillingness to give up one iota of the rights of his community and rejected those parts of Khaddam's paper that, in his estimate, would turn the president into a "chief clerk." He then suggested that if the Muslims considered the proposed terms of reference of the president and the prime minister fair and equitable, they could take the positions of president and speaker of parliament and leave the posts of prime minister and president of the proposed senate to the Christians. Franjieh's proposal was rejected by the Lebanese Front. Further meetings between Khaddam, Franjieh, and the Muslim coalition failed to result in any progress.

The Gracious Way Out

It became evident that internal differences were both significant and explosive and that the conferees were in no mood or position to make concessions. The conference then turned its attention to find a face-saving mechanism to end the talks. Nabih Barri suggested that the conference take decisions on security and disengagement arrangements and then adjourn to allow time for further exploration and consultation, because ideological differences between confessional and nonconfessional schemes could not be resolved in one day. Camille Chamoun also called for adjournment after agreeing on a cease-fire and on the formation of a national unity government that would form a commission to draft within one year a new constitution based on unity, justice, and equality. Khaddam, though bitter and disillusioned, counseled against any statement that might give the impression that the national dialogue had reached a deadlock, because a stalemate would lead Lebanon and the region into a dark tunnel of unknown consequences.

The final communiqué was an obituary in pleasant terms, to use Khaddam's words. It gave the impression that enough progress had been made to require the formation of a commission of specialists in law and politics to draft a new constitution. Additional resolutions included (1) a cease-fire and the formulation of a security plan; (2) the formation of a high level political-military commission to oversee the implementation of the security plan; (3) the termination of all hostile media campaigns; and (4) continuous consultations among members of the national dialogue group and future meetings upon the invitation of the president.

16

Phase X. Restitution of the Syrian Initiative (1984)

The conventional wisdom after the abrogation of the Lebanese-Israeli troop withdrawal agreement and the improvement of Lebanese-Syrian relations was that agreement on internal issues would be quick and easy. On the contrary, eight days of intensive talks in Lausanne proved that internal differences were so deep rooted in communal traditions that even the political leaders themselves did not have enough maneuverability to strike compromises and avoid an impasse. Lausanne, however, was only the beginning of a new Syrian policy governed by three overriding principles. First, violence and armed confrontation would not be encouraged or allowed as a mechanism to settle political and communal differences or shape the future of Lebanon. The political life that was halted in the aftermath of the May 17 Agreement was to be resumed. Syria had no reason any more to support armed opposition to the government. Israel, as well, for domestic and external reasons, was neither willing nor ready to support the implications of the "new opposition" of the Lebanese Forces. Second, internal differences were so interlocked and intrinsic that only a strong external mediator like Syria could bring about an accord among the Lebanese. The unsuccessful brokerage in Lausanne should be considered an accidental setback and not a substantive manifestation of ineffectiveness. Third, Damascus wished to complete the success of the "Syrian option" by negating every success that Israel and the United States had achieved in Lebanon and return to the status it had enjoyed before the Israeli invasion of 1982. It also needed to make the Syrian option succeed where other options failed. On both counts, Israeli withdrawal became a high priority objective for Syria in Lebanon.

The reentry of the Syrian political initiative into Lebanese affairs was viewed with certain unease by the Druze and Shi'a, who saw it as a damper on their ambition to translate their military victories into commensurate political gains. The Lebanese Forces and their allies openly opposed what they called, the Syrianization of Lebanon. Later on, however, they came to realize that neither the United States nor Israel were viable options anymore and that close cooperation with Syria was Lebanon's only option – and perhaps the Christians' only safeguard of their rights.

Within the context of the above objectives and developments Syrian-Lebanese cooperation concentrated on the revival of the Lebanese political process and the achievement of national *entente*, the security and restoration of state sovereignty, and the withdrawal of Israeli troops.

Internal *Entente*

The dialogue on political reform did not end in Lausanne and was resumed in a series of meetings in Beirut and Damascus with various Lebanese leaders, culminating in a summit meeting between Presidents Gemayel and Assad on April 19, 1984, in which both leaders agreed on a reform document to serve as a guideline for drafting a new constitution by the constitutional commission decided upon in Lausanne. The document was essentially Khaddam's Lausanne working paper, with two major modifications: Instead of considering the cabinet the highest executive and administrative authority, the document reaffirmed the constitutional principle that the president of the republic was the head of the executive branch. The document also institutionalized the tradition of power distribution between the president and the prime minister.

On the basis of the reform document to which the political leaders subscribed, a government of national unity, headed by Rashid Karami and including leaders of the Lebanese Front and the opposition, was formed on April 30. After some delays, the cabinet appointed the constitutional committee in September 1984 to draft a new constitution. It is not as large as the Lausanne conference proposed, but it is representative and, as of January 1985, was hard at work.

Security and State Sovereignty

Immediately after Lausanne, the political-security committee resolved upon was formed under the president's chairmanship. The committee, and later the government, succeeded with Syrian assistance in establishing a satisfactory degree of security followed by disengagement of forces along the Beirut green line. The extension of state authority into militia-controlled areas, however, implied the deployment of the army, which for many years had not been accepted in Muslim circles on the ground that it was confessionally unbalanced. To improve the army's acceptability, the leadership was changed and the structure was modified to make it more of a collective command. Even then, it took Syrian arm-twisting before the government could agree on a security plan to deploy the army along the coastal road to the Awwali River in the south and Batrun in the north.

Meanwhile, attempts continued to maintain and even broaden the political support for the government. Syria had used its influence with Nabih Barri and Walid Junblat to support the government and cooperate with the president – a posture that could threaten their popularity within their respective communities. On the Christian side, President Gemayel consolidated his position in the Kata'ib Party after the death of his father and party leader on August 29, 1984 and succeeded in bringing the Lebanese Forces, with a new leadership, back under party control.

Withdrawal of Israeli Troops

The government of national unity took the traditional Arab line in dealing with Israel. It closed the Israeli liaison office near Beirut and endorsed the resistance to Israeli occupation in the south. Moreover, assaults on Israeli soldiers and the Israeli-backed southern Lebanon Army – now commanded by General Antoine Lahad, Sa'ad Haddad's successor – increased as the resistance movement developed into a significant force of two dimensions: Shi'a – demonstrated by the support of religious leaders and the involvement of Amal – and ideological – demonstrated by the participation of the Communist organizations and the Syrian Social National Party.

The Lebanese government, however, maintained its commitment to "security arrangements and measures that provide sovereignty and security in Southern Lebanon, prevent infiltration across the southern border, and secure the withdrawal of Israeli forces."[18] Syria had approved this notion, but was not in favor of the direct negotiations that Israel was demanding. Both Lebanon and Syria wanted the United States to broker a security arrangements agreement with Israel, and in early October, Rashid Karami appealed to Secretary of State Shultz, asking that the United States participate in arranging for the withdrawal of the IDF. Later in the month, Israel joined in inviting U.S. mediation to achieve security guarantees. Washington declined on the ground that more flexibility and a change of mood must be exhibited by the parties concerned – Syria, Israel, and Lebanon – before such an effort could be undertaken.

Meanwhile, the Israeli government officially dropped its demand for a simultaneous Syrian withdrawal and on October 17, 1984, Shimon Peres's office issued the new conditions for a complete Israeli withdrawal from Lebanon:

1. A Syrian commitment not to move troops into areas vacated by the IDF;
2. A Syrian commitment to prevent guerrilla infiltration toward Israel from Syrian-controlled territory;
3. The continued deployment of Major Haddad's succes-

sor, Antoine Lahad's Southern Lebanon Army, in an unde-
fined zone adjacent to the border.

4. A redeployment of UNIFIL north of Lahad's deployment zone in an area stretching between the Lebanese coast
and the Syrian border.

Dealing with these conditions required reaching an understanding with Syria and an agreement with Lebanon.
Washington agreed to play a low profile role between Syria
and Israel, the extent of which would be a function of the
cooperation of the two parties. The Lebanese-Israeli discussions were started on November 8, 1984 in the form of a "conference of military representatives" under the auspices of the
UN – a compromise between the Lebanese demand for a revival of the armistice committee and the Israeli demand for
direct negotiations.

The present discussions are in many respects a rerun of
the earlier negotiations that ended with the May 17 Agreement. Israel's familiar formula for security based on friendly
local forces and the right of hot pursuit has been countered
by Lebanon's familiar insistence on the Lebanese Army as
the sole security agent based on the argument that a modest
force operating in a friendly environment and among cooper-
ating local residents can be more effective than heavily armed
troops operating in a hostile environment. The progress in
these discussions is closely linked to Israel's political agenda.
It is also indirectly dependent upon Syria's decision about
some withdrawal or redeployment, because an Israeli withdrawal on the basis of an agreement that has Syria's consent
would leave little justification for Damascus not to reciprocate with a significant withdrawal.

There is consensus in Lebanon, ranging from enthusiasm
to grudging acceptance, that the Syrian initiative is the only
viable option for the country. There are high hopes that Syria,
for its own prestige, will try earnestly to bring overall stability to Lebanon and foster national *entente*. Alternatively,
there are worries that Lebanon may pay for its association
with Syria in the evolving regional struggle if Egypt and Jor-

dan try to stir up trouble for Syria or Syria moves against Jordan. Moreover, if the peace process should get underway with King Hussein and Yasir Arafat, Israel might use Lebanon to create problems for Syria. The obvious question is whether the Syrian option can succeed where other options have failed and restore to Lebanon its unity, sovereignty, and territorial integrity. Maybe this is the wrong question, one that reflects a Lebanese political culture that is partially responsible for the failure of external initiatives. A more appropriate question might be whether Lebanon, with its traditional external relations and the special contacts it acquired over the past two years, can reciprocate to Syria for its initiative and thus transfer Syria's role from a political godfather to a partner in a profitable joint venture for peace and stability.

III

Conclusions

17

Future Directions

Is There Hope?

It is clear from the previous sections that Lebanon is beset
with problems whose magnitude has engulfed the state —
issues of identity that go to the heart of the state, pressures
that have resulted from the turbulence and violence of the
Arab-Israeli conflict, strains that have come from a dynamic
political environment wrestling with a traditional political
system, and problems that have derived from the prolonged
absence of the state's effective operation on its national territory. The monumental extent of these problems has led to
a number of initiatives to restore Lebanese sovereignty and
reconstruct Lebanon's polity, society, and economy. All of
these initiatives have failed.

Two conclusions about Lebanon's future may be drawn
from this tragic experience. The first is that the Lebanese
state is not viable, that it is a political fiction — a geographic
creation with no real constituency. Alternatively, but of the
same policy direction, some have concluded that Lebanon's
problems are too many, too great, and too complex for solution and that the resulting conflict vortex sucks in and weak-
ens all who attempt to help — Syria in 1976, Israel in 1982,

the MNF, and the United States. These are not unreasonable views, based upon experiential evidence.

There is an alternative conclusion, however: Lebanon's case is not hopeless. This view recognizes that Lebanon is a developing country and, like many others, is suffering the ailments of the maturation process, as its long history of communal autonomy, intermittent conflict, and traditional leadership patterns clash with the pressure of modernization. Lebanon is going through a traumatic period and undoubtedly will continue to experience pain as it struggles to establish an optimal formula that will reflect Lebanese culture in all its political, economic, and social diversity and still provide stability.

Structural tensions cannot realistically or adequately be portrayed as having mutually exclusive properties of conflict or resolution. These stresses reflect the pressures that even the most mature political systems confront: the search for a balance between stability and change. Any system that provides one to the exclusion of the other will disappear, but the balance between the two is dynamic and particularly difficult to establish at the early stages of political development.

To conclude that Lebanon's future is necessarily bright would be engaging in fantasy, but to conclude the reverse is no less fatuous. It has always been easy to extrapolate on a linear basis from the present, be it the present of 1955 or that of 1985, and conclude that the future is "more of the same." Yet, ultimately, it is never more of the same forever, and I have tried to point out factors that augur for change, whether for good or ill. It is interesting to note that the same elements that resist change in the short term are also those that assure it over the long term, and that this is true both internally and externally. Under these circumstances, while the Lebanese may enjoy less control over their destiny at present than ever before, their own aggregate behavior (by which I mean ways of thinking as much as ways of acting) in the years ahead will likely determine the future of Lebanon.

Although the Lebanese criticize each other and their political system, despite the depth of their views they all seek to change the system while preserving Lebanon. No Lebanese leader seeks partition or advocates the annexation of part or all of Lebanon to Syria or Israel. Why? What has held the Lebanese together since 1920 is the common belief, one that has cut across all religious communities, in a democratic way of life based upon cooperation and interdependence. These common values underlie Lebanon's political system and accurately reflect the shared interests and expectations and aspirations of all communities. It is clear, then, that any formula intended to resolve Lebanon's problems must be constructed around the principle of a united, distinct, and sovereign Lebanon.

There are also some reasons for optimism over the conflicting interests of Lebanon's powerful neighbors. Israel appears to have no long-term territorial ambitions in Lebanon, and Israeli policy favors withdrawal for at least four reasons. First, domestic Israeli public opinion overwhelmingly favors withdrawal. Second, the foreign policy of Israel, despite its coalition government, reflects a consensus that Lebanon poses no threat to Israel's survival, that the security of northern Israel does not require a continuous military presence in southern Lebanon, and that the political configuration and tenor of Lebanon are not crucial to Israel as long as Lebanon does not become a confrontation state and allow its territory to be used for aggression against Israel. Third, withdrawal from Lebanon appears to be prerequisite to reducing some of the social divisions in Israel. Fourth, the cost of continued occupation is high for the beleaguered Israeli economy, especially in view of the costs to the country in terms of social programs. From the positions advanced by various Israeli officials, it is apparent that Israel now accepts the Arab character of Lebanon and would be prepared to accept substantial Syrian influence (as was the case in 1976), especially if such a situation facilitated the attainment of a guarantee for the security of Israel's northern border.

Syrian interests, too, can be met well short of the loss of Lebanese territory or sovereignty. Syria has three principal interests in Lebanon. The primary concern is security.

Damascus seeks to ensure that no plots directed against Syria are launched from Lebanon. The second set of interests is economic. In this respect, transit and water rights (the latter particularly concerning the Assi [Orontes] River) play a prominent role. Third, Syrian leaders hope to use Lebanon as an asset in negotiations on the larger Arab-Israeli problem. In spite of the historically close relationship between Lebanon and Syria, none of these interests requires a physical Syrian presence in Lebanon. Only in the north, where many armed Palestinian elements are located, may Syria feel compelled to remain. All Syria's needs (except perhaps control of the Palestinians) can be met with a friendly government in Beirut. In fact, the more dependable that government the greater Syria's incentive to withdraw, because withdrawal would reduce Syrian vulnerabilities, especially if the conflict with Egypt, Iraq, and Jordan continues to escalate.

It must be clear from the recent past that a physical presence in Lebanon is unnecessary and even counterproductive for both Israel and Syria in terms of the Arab-Israeli conflict. Lebanon is too weak to challenge Israel (or to assist Syria). Lebanon has never been a party to the conflict, but for 15 years has been a field on which the conflict has been played out. To this extent, real and substantial progress toward a general settlement is very much in the long-term interests of Lebanon, though in the short term the strains associated with the process may well increase conflict in Lebanon if Israeli and Syrian forces do not withdraw.

It is also encouraging that although the recent U.S. initiative in Lebanon after the 1982 war ended in mutual frustration and bitterness, the political relation survived. The United States is still committed to the restoration of Lebanese unity, sovereignty, and territorial integrity. On the other hand, although certain elements in Lebanon seek complete U.S. disengagement as a result of attacks on U.S. personnel, all the mainstream groups agree on one thing: they want to see the United States in Lebanon in a peacemaking role.

Conflict Resolution

The multidimensionality of the conflict in Lebanon must be reflected in efforts at conflict resolution. Such efforts must be judged in terms of their response to the four interactive issues raised in the first chapter – Lebanon's identity, the Lebanese political system, the Arab-Israeli conflict, and Lebanon's sovereignty. The social and psychological dimensions are no less necessary to address than the political, economic, and military or security dimensions. The multidimensionality must also extend in space as well as time – it must realistically take account of Israeli and Syrian concerns that Lebanon not become a launching pad for hostile acts, whether political or military, directed against their interests, nor lose its autonomy to a hostile power. It must be evident that the concept of security, which in its broadest sense incorporates economic, social, political, and military variables, dominates all others – communal security, Lebanese security, Israeli security, Syrian security. At the same time, it must also be evident that no single party inside or outside Lebanon can be, or be seen to be, the victor if the situation is to stabilize. The explanation for this reasoning is the old political adage that complete security for one party means complete insecurity for another. The distance between minimum and maximum positions is often exactly equal to the value of – and incentive to respect – the status quo.

The four elements that are critical to the transformation of hope for Lebanon into the reality of a peaceful, stable Lebanon are the insulation of the country, the establishment of a strong national government, administrative decentralization, and the modernization of the state.

Insulation of Lebanon from the Arab-Israeli conflict is a primary principle that serves the interests of all parties. Israel will benefit from the reduction of Syrian influence and removal of Syrian armed presence in Lebanon, Syria from the creation in Lebanon of a real buffer zone that will prevent Israel from circumventing Syria's defenses on the Golan and that will preclude the outbreak of hostilities in Lebanon between Syrian and Israeli forces. Syria is already protected by a treaty with the Soviet Union against an Israeli attack on Syria. Nor are the benefits of insulation limited to the territory of the Lebanese state. Both superpowers will also profit. The United States, which has faced some of its gravest crises in the Middle East and has come closest there to a direct confrontation with the USSR, can gain relief from the substantial reduction in Arab-Israeli tension that neutralization would mean. And just as these crises have impelled regional governments to turn to the United States because of its unique relationship with Israel, the Soviet Union will certainly gain if there is no further major involvement of the United States in the Middle East such as occurred after the wars of 1973 and 1982.

Internally as well such insulation offers major benefits. It would encourage Muslim and Christian to be Lebanese and Arab without the danger of opting, with this identity, for isolation or compromising Lebanon's sovereignty to any party in the Arab-Israeli conflict and without suffering society-rending pressures from two belligerent neighbors. The Lebanese system, overtaxed by the multitude of pressures placed on it, will be able to focus on Lebanese national issues rather than developments well beyond its capacity for influence.

We are not proposing any specific type of insulation, which can take many forms. These forms range from de facto insulation based on a tacit accord, through national decisions formalized by Lebanon's constitution, to multilateral action in the Arab League, and to international agreements reached at the level of the United Nations.

At the national level, a strong central government that is also a fair central government is the key to security for all the Lebanese. Only such a government can assure the law and order that are as critical to security as fairness is. The point at issue is to create an executive authority that has real power but does not threaten the interests of any group of the major components of the state. The 1943 National Pact was intended to do just that — ensuring that the three largest communities (far larger than any others and which, today still constitute more than 70 percent of the population) occupied the three critical executive positions — "presidencies" of the state, the government, and the Parliament. Nevertheless, it is apparent that public confidence in the equitability of this approach has collapsed and therefore that it must be replaced by a system that enjoys greater faith and still assures the executive representation of at least as great a proportion of the public.

The central national government of Lebanon must certainly be reformed, and indeed all communities have long recognized this necessity. Discussions during and after the Lausanne talks reflect the universal acceptance of the concept of structural reform. All communities approve the principle of equitable and broader participation in national government. The changing social order in Lebanon that is propelling new leaders and new groupings to the fore must also be taken into account in the process of broadening participatory democracy. When government responds to the people, people respond to the government. The questions of centralization and power distribution are intensely interactive. Those favoring shifts in power distribution oppose decentralization, and, although decentralization is seen as a reasonable compromise by others, it is attacked as a form of preserving the economic status quo.

One means to resolve these problems is to marry political and economic goals. This approach would accept decentralization as a realistic step to be taken in conjunction with a redistribution of political power — but only when accompanied by additional measures designed to modify the extreme distribution of income and foster real and equitably dispersed development. All communities in fact insist on a degree of administrative decentralization because of their strong sectarian and other values that can best be nurtured in an environment in which the state does not impose itself in many local affairs. Similarly, all Lebanon will benefit from real economic reforms that give every community and every region the incentive to preserve and support the government and state.

The Lebanese have concentrated so intensely on their own experience they have been too slow to look elsewhere for relevant experience. Many heterogeneous states have had to address problems akin to those in Lebanon. The once-dominant but not-forgotten rivalry between large and small states led to a U.S. federal system that has certainly demonstrated ample central government strength to ensure law and order and security, all the while leaving to the states and local jurisdictions wide latitude in many matters. There are numerous lessons that can be drawn from the experience of many countries where implementation of central government decisions is local and others where administrative decisions are made locally.

A key to the viability of any new formula must be not only its equitableness, which must be a prerequisite to adoption in any case, but also to its success in promoting and dispersing development. For this reason the most critical elements of reform are at least as much in the administrative and economic arenas as they are in the political domain. Decentralization must certainly be balanced or limited by mechanisms to redistribute income such that development levels are not frozen. It is a matter of great concern that, although Lebanon has historically had the highest skills base and educational level in the Arab Middle East and although the human factor is certainly the key to development, Lebanon has been stagnating in contrast with many other states of the area.

Equally important is modernization. The Lebanese are remarkable in their ability to modernize their approaches to all forms of business and professional practices, but equally remarkable in their resistance to modernization of political and administrative practices. The nature of contemporary society, highlighted by the attention of the communications media on all areas, demands a replacement of patron-client relations by meritocracy. With Lebanon's wealth of human resources, the individual and the society will both be far better served by such a modernization of the public sector. Modernization is important in and of itself in improving the quality of life, but it is at least as critical as a demonstration of what the state can bring to its citizens.

Modernization will necessarily entail major social changes as well as political ones. The improvement of management procedures and decision-making processes to ensure equality under the law must mean not only that all receive their due irrespective of who they are, but, just as important, that none receives more than his due irrespective of who he is. Such a change – no less than revolutionary in Lebanon – will reduce the dependence on traditional leaders and the need for communal endorsement.

A major element in modernization is to replace personal leadership with dynamic institutions. These institutions must contribute to administrative development and should rationalize and streamline national decision making and action in such endeavors as national planning, research and development, management, and manpower training. The primary functions of the state, including development, must become a continuous professional activity rather than behavior directed by discontinuous political tactics.

There is no single answer to the complex of issues that have victimized the Lebanese, just as there is no single explanation of the causes of the conflict. Yet, it seems that any formula designed to restore peace to Lebanon must address the fundamental crises of identity, the sectarian divisions, the Arab-Israeli conflict, and the challenges to sovereignty. To overlook any of these four principal issues is to ensure they will again all conspire to produce conflict. The guidelines suggested here – a combination of insulation at the international level, broader participation at the national level, decentralization of many domestic functions, and institutional reforms and modernization to ensure the protection of the primary interests of each community and the vitality and equitability of a developmental dynamic – seem to be critical elements in determining the modalities that will realize the

Lebanese national will to restore the unity of the country while protecting it from the overzealous concerns of other regional powers.

Notes

1. Halim Barakat, *Lebanon in Strife* (Austin, Texas: University of Texas Press, 1977), 31.

2. Kamal Junblat, *This Is My Will* (Paris: Muassassat al-Watan al-Arabi, 1978), 78, 94 (Arabic).

3. Shaykh Hasan Khalid, *Muslims in Lebanon and the Civil War* (Beirut: Dar al-Kindi, 1978), 282 (Arabic).

4. From a speech delivered by the representative of the "Front of Rejectionist Forces" in a fighter's funeral in Tel al-Za'atar and quoted in *An-Nahar*, March 8, 1976.

5. Political editor of WAFA (Palestinian News Agency) as quoted in *An-Nahar*, June 4, 1976.

6. Nayif Hawatmeh in *Contemporary Issues* 1, no. 4 (July 1970): 6–7.

7. *An-Nahar*, March 10, 1976.

8. George Hawi, secretary general of the Lebanese Communist Party in *An-Nahar*, February 27, 1976.

9. *As-Safir*, April 16, 1980.

10. *An-Nahar*, May 13, 1982.

11. Ze'ev Schiff and Ehud Ya'ari, *Israel's Lebanon War* (New York, N.Y.: Simon and Schuster, 1984), 42.

12. Ibid., 45–55.

13. Ibid., 51.

14. Ibid., 236–237.

15. The minutes of Geneva and Lausanne meetings have been published in Arabic in *Geneva-Lausanne – The Full Secret Minutes*

(Beirut: Arab Information Center, 1984) and *Confessional Princes* (Beirut: Central Information Agency, 1984).

16. From President Gemayel's opening address to the national dialogue conference in Lausanne, March 12, 1984.

17. From the minutes of the Lausanne meeting.

18. Part of the cabinet decision of March 5, 1984 by which the May 17 Agreement was abrogated.